LIFE PICTURE PUZZLE

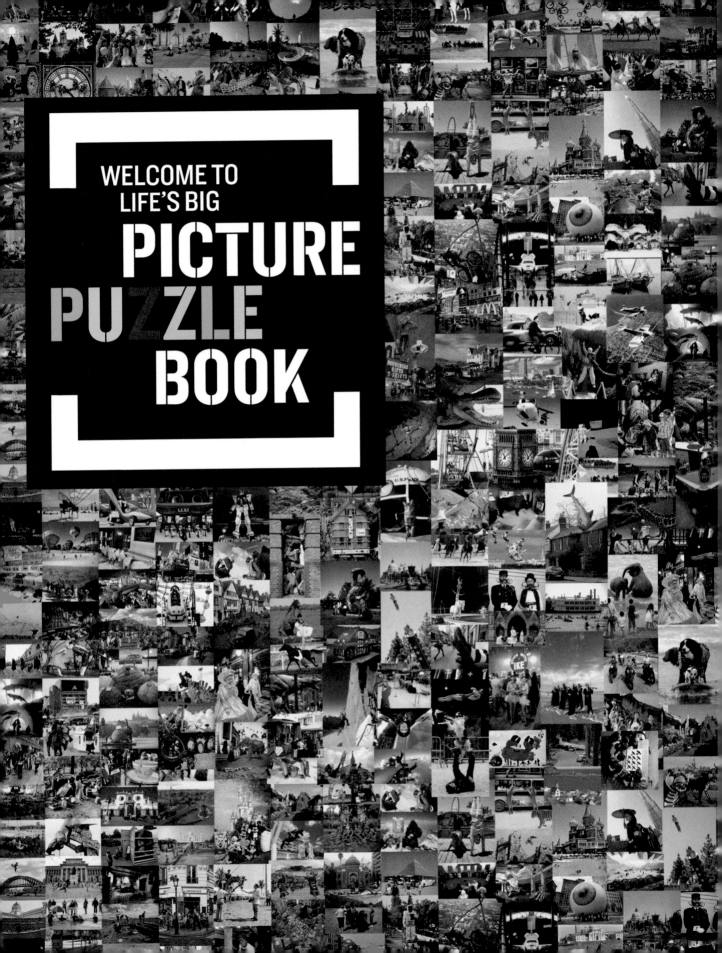

WELCOME TO
LIFE'S BIG
PICTURE
PUZZLE
BOOK

LIFE PICTURE PUZZLE

Puzzle Master Michael Roseman
Editor Robert Sullivan
Director of Photography Barbara Baker Burrows
Deputy Picture Editor Christina Lieberman
Photo Associate Sarah Cates
Copy Editors Danielle Dowling, Marilyn Fu, Barbara Gogan

LIFE Puzzle Books
Managing Editor Bill Shapiro

Editorial Operations

Richard K. Prue (Director), Brian Fellows (Manager), Keith Aurelio, Charlotte Coco, Kevin Hart, Mert Kerimoglu, Rosalie Khan, Patricia Koh, Marco Lau, Brian Mai, Po Fung Ng, Rudi Papiri, Robert Pizaro, Barry Pribula, Clara Renauro, Katy Saunders, Samantha Schwendeman, Hia Tan, Vaune Trachtman

Time Home Entertainment
Publisher Jim Childs
Vice President, Business Development & Strategy Steven Sandonato
Executive Director, Marketing Services Carol Pittard
Executive Director, Retail & Special Sales Tom Mifsud
Executive Publishing Director Joy Butts
Director, Bookazine Development & Marketing Laura Adam
Finance Director Glenn Buonocore
Associate Publishing Director Megan Pearlman
Assistant General Counsel Helen Wan
Assistant Director, Special Sales Ilene Schreider
Book Production Manager Suzanne Janso
Design & Prepress Manager Anne-Michelle Gallero
Brand Manager Roshni Patel
Associate Prepress Manager Alex Voznesenskiy
Assistant Brand Manager Stephanie Braga

Editorial Director Stephen Koepp
Editorial Operations Director Michael Q. Bullerdick

Special thanks to Christine Austin, Katherine Barnet, Jeremy Biloon, Susan Chodakiewicz, Rose Cirrincione, Lauren Hall Clark, Jacqueline Fitzgerald, Christine Font, Jenna Goldberg, Hillary Hirsch, David Kahn, Amy Mangus, Robert Marasco, Kimberly Marshall, Amy Migliaccio, Nina Mistry, Dave Rozzelle, Adriana Tierno, Vanessa Wu

PUBLISHED BY

LIFE Books

an imprint of Time Home Entertainment Inc.

Copyright © 2012
Time Home Entertainment Inc.
135 West 50th Street
New York, NY 10020

ISBN 13: 978-1-60320-403-3
ISBN 10: 1-60320-403-2

We welcome your comments and suggestions about LIFE Books. Please write to us at:
LIFE Books
Attention: Book Editors
PO Box 11016
Des Moines, IA 50336-1016

If you would like to order any of our hardcover Collector's Edition books, please call us at 1-800-327-6388 (Monday through Friday, 7 a.m. to 8 p.m., or Saturday, 7 a.m. to 6 p.m. Central Time).

COVER PHOTO: STR/AFP/GETTY

One Small Step

But if either astronaut actually moves, run for your lives!

✳ ✳ ✳
✳ ✳ ✳
✳

STEPHEN JAFFE/AFP/GETTY

7
changes

KEEP
SCORE

3min 55sec

A — B — C — D — E

1 | 2 | 3 | 4 | 5

You'll notice that we like to start off nice and easy.

ANSWERS No. 1 (A2): They've added extra ventilation for the crowds. **No. 2 (A2 to B2):** NASA briefly experimented with Mood Visors™ but they left the astronauts feeling a bit blue. **No. 3 (A4):** This star spins widdershins. **No. 4 (C2):** When no one is looking, a plaque rises slowly up the wall. **No. 5 (C3 to E5):** Betsy Ross would flip over these stripes. **No. 6 (D2):** Trust us, this doesn't count as a bigfoot sighting. **No. 7 (D3):** The lander has one fewer leg to stand on.

Please Bless These Climbers

And may they also have all the hot cocoa they can drink

DOUG ALLAN/THE IMAGE BANK/GETTY

9 changes

KEEP SCORE

5min 15sec

A — B — C — D — E

1 | 2 | 3 | 4 | 5

After you master these puzzles, get ready for some real challenges!

ANSWERS No. 1 (A3): Red flag at base camp, climbers take care. **No. 2 (B3 to C3):** They call me Mr. Swivel-Hips. **Nos. 3 and 4 (B4):** These two guys are cap buddies now, while the pole has staged a strategic retreat. **No. 5 (C1 to C2):** Who wears puffy pants? He wears puffy pants. **No. 6 (C2):** He's a just little transparent, isn't he? **No. 7 (D1):** If there's going to be soda on Mount Everest, shouldn't it be Mountain Dew? **No. 8 (D3):** His cup didn't runneth over, it just disappeared. **No. 9 (E1):** The thermos wants to be part of the group.

READY, SET, GO!

LIFE AROUND THE WORLD

PICTURE PUZZLE

SEQUEL TO THE #1 NEW YORK TIMES BEST-SELLER

CAN YOU SPOT THE DIFFERENCES?

THE 10TH BOOK IN THE WILDLY POPULAR SERIES
4 LEVELS: NOVICE · MASTER · EXPERT · GENIUS

WELCOME TO LIFE'S TENTH PICTURE PUZZLE BOOK

Here we are, less than five years after publishing our first Picture Puzzle book, and we find ourselves already at our 10th! We'll be honest: When we invented these puzzle books we never expected that the response would be so overwhelming that we might have to keep the presses running—and our puzzle masters hard at work—almost constantly. But the letters and e-mails keep pouring in, asking for more puzzles. We're only too happy to comply: These Picture Puzzle books are fun to work on. And now we have 10.

To celebrate this milestone, we figured we needed a big theme. We had already traveled across America in one book and looked at holidays in another, dealt with animals in a third, and, in our last volume, presented a book's worth of mysteries drawn from old movies and TV shows. What now, for big No. 10? Well, why not traverse the whole wide world?

And so we do, sailing the seven seas and visiting every hemisphere. We have brought changes to famous sites like the Eiffel Tower, seen on our cover, and to out-of-the-way secrets known only to the locals. As always, we have tried to choose the most vivid, most colorful, most fun photographs. This book will make any puzzle player happy, and it's also a cheerful travelogue.

Our 10th book captures what's best about the whole series, and everything you loved about our earlier books is still here. Our Novice section sets an easy pace so you can ramp up your skills as you go. Our Master and Expert sections incrementally add to the challenge, and when you tackle our Genius puzzles, you'll be a certified puzzle master yourself.

But you already knew all that. You're familiar with how our books proceed. You've been with us a long time now. Ten whole books.

And counting!

[OUR CUT-UP PUZZLES: EASY AS 1-2-3]

We snipped a photo into four or six pieces. Then we rearranged the pieces and numbered them.

Your mission: Beneath each cut-up puzzle, write the number of the piece in the box where it belongs.

Check the answer key at the back of the book to see what the reassembled image looks like.

[HOW TO PLAY THE PUZZLES]

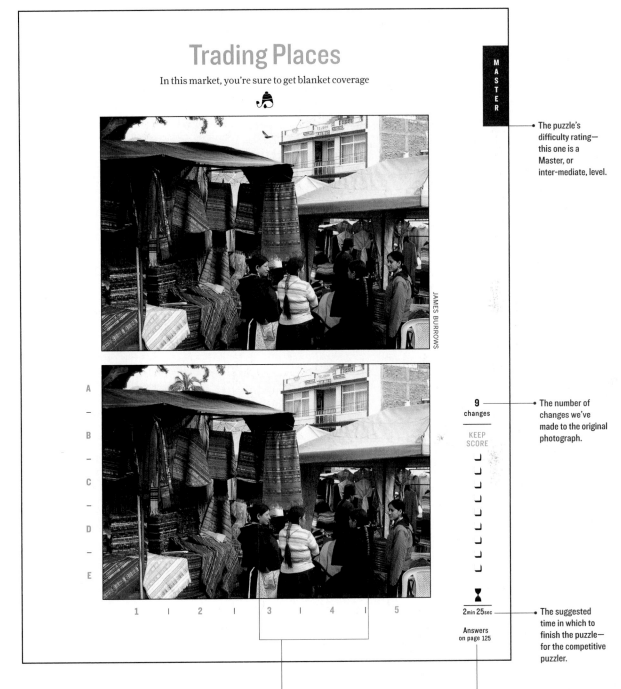

Trading Places

In this market, you're sure to get blanket coverage

MASTER

The puzzle's difficulty rating—this one is a Master, or inter-mediate, level.

JAMES BURROWS

9
changes

The number of changes we've made to the original photograph.

KEEP SCORE

2min 25sec

The suggested time in which to finish the puzzle—for the competitive puzzler.

Answers on page 125

The differences between pictures can range from the relatively obvious to the maddeningly subtle, depending on the difficulty rating. For instance, one of these ladies has lost an earring, while another is sporting a braid of a different color. Seven more changes are left to spot in this puzzle.

The page on which the answers can be found. Use the numbered and lettered grid to help you find any changes you might have missed.

NOVICE

[
These puzzles are for everyone:
rookies and veterans,
young and old. Start here, and
sharpen your skills.
]

Like Clockwork

Big Ben usually gets the time right three times out of four

1

2

3

4

DAN CHUNG/REUTERS/CORBIS

0min 35sec

Answer
on page 125

Way Beyond Frosty

Kids in Ottawa don't settle for snowmen

CARL & ANN PURCELL/CORBIS

A
–
B
–
C
–
D
–
E

1 | 2 | 3 | 4 | 5

8
changes

⧗

2min 10sec

Answers
on page 125

KEEP SCORE ★ ❏ ❏ ❏ ❏ ❏ ❏ ❏ ❏

Totally Digging Colorado

Will these archaeologists find any buried treasure at Shields Pueblo? Will you?

STEFANO AMANTINI/CORBIS

A
—
B
—
C
—
D
—
E

1   2   3   4   5

7
changes

⧗
2min 20sec

Answers
on page 125

Pegasus

Pigs might not fly in England, but horses do

LEO MASON/CORBIS

A
—
B
—
C
—
D
—
E

1   2   3   4   5

8
changes

⧗

2 min 30 sec

Answers
on page 125

KEEP SCORE ★ ❑ ❑ ❑ ❑ ❑ ❑ ❑ ❑

Frozen Dinner

At Japan's high-end Alpha Resort Tomamu, cold is hot

1

2

3

4

5

6

0min 55sec

Answer
on page 125

KIM KYUNG-HOON/REUTERS/CORBIS

Midday March

Which one of these photos has an off-color parade participant?

1

2

3

4

5

6

EMILY PRESCOTT

0min 45sec

Answer
on page 125

Rolling Along

In Newport Beach, California, Segway is *your* way

A

B

C

D

E

1   2   3   4   5

7
changes

2min 25sec

Answers
on page 125

KEEP SCORE ★ ❏ ❏ ❏ ❏ ❏ ❏ ❏

Busman's Holiday

The tigers at Seoul's safari park want a look, too

PAUL CHESLEY/GETTY

A
B
C
D
E

1   2   3   4   5

8
changes

⏳
2min 30sec

Answers
on page 125

KEEP SCORE ★ ❏ ❏ ❏ ❏ ❏ ❏ ❏ ❏

Dutch Treat

This landscape is shifting with the wind

FABFOTO/GETTY

A

B

C

D

E

1 2 3 4 5

7
changes

2min 40sec

Answers
on page 125

KEEP SCORE ★ ❏ ❏ ❏ ❏ ❏ ❏ ❏

Dracula Slept Here

In Romania, remember to *count* the changes. *Mwa-ha-ha!*

WOJTEK LASKI/GETTY

A
—
B
—
C
—
D
—
E

1 | 2 | 3 | 4 | 5

7
changes

⧗
3min 30sec

Answers
on page 126

KEEP SCORE ★ ❏ ❏ ❏ ❏ ❏ ❏ ❏

Do You Buy?

Nowadays in Dubai, the answer is probably "No"

INSY SHAH/GETTY

A
—
B
—
C
—
D
—
E

1 | 2 | 3 | 4 | 5

7
changes

⏳

2min 5sec

Answers
on page 126

KEEP SCORE ★ ❑ ❑ ❑ ❑ ❑ ❑ ❑

Buzz Off

Flying insects on the beach in Perth can be such a nuisance

PAUL KANE/GETTY

A
–
B
–
C
–
D
–
E

1 | 2 | 3 | 4 | 5

7
changes

⧗
1min 55sec

Answers
on page 126

KEEP SCORE ★ ❏ ❏ ❏ ❏ ❏ ❏ ❏

Head Over Heels

At Sea World in Australia, everyone's flippin'

A

B

C

D

E

1   2   3   4   5

8
changes

KEEP
SCORE!

❏
❏
❏
❏
❏
❏
❏
❏

⌛
2min 40sec

Answers
on page 126

Baaaah!

Life is woolly in Vermont

MELANIE STETSON FREEMAN/CHRISTIAN SCIENCE MONITOR/GETTY

A
—
B
—
C
—
D
—
E

1   2   3   4   5

8 changes

⏳ 2min 15sec

Answers on page 126

KEEP SCORE ★ ❏ ❏ ❏ ❏ ❏ ❏ ❏ ❏

The Sky's the Limit

Keep an eye on these rascally rockets in New Mexico

A
—
B
—
C
—
D
—
E

1   2   3   4   5

LIFE

6
changes

⧗
1min 45sec

Answers
on page 126

KEEP SCORE ★ ❏ ❏ ❏ ❏ ❏ ❏

Where's Santa?

On the Russian Steppes, reindeer await the big guy's call

A
—
B
—
C
—
D
—
E

1   2   3   4   5

5
changes

1min **45**sec

Answers
on page 126

KEEP SCORE ★ ❏ ❏ ❏ ❏ ❏

Making Merry

Camera phones are mandatory at Merryland in Guilin, China

PER ANDERS PETTERSSON/GETTY

A

B

C

D

E

1   2   3   4   5

8
changes

⧗
2min 05sec

Answers
on page 126

KEEP SCORE ★ ❏ ❏ ❏ ❏ ❏ ❏ ❏ ❏

Chillin' in Southern California

The penguins at San Diego's Sea World are on the march toward her magic chum bucket

A
—
B
—
C
—
D
—
E

1   2   3   4   5

6
changes

⏳

2min 15sec

Answers
on page 126

KEEP SCORE ★ ❏ ❏ ❏ ❏ ❏ ❏

Olé

Can you spot the changes made to this bullring in Seville, Spain?

A
–
B
–
C
–
D
–
E

1 2 3 4 5

6
changes

⏳

2min 55sec

Answers
on page 126

KEEP SCORE ★ ❑ ❑ ❑ ❑ ❑ ❑

MASTER

[
Here, puzzles get
a little harder. You'll
need to raise
your game a level.
]

Mirror Image

Everything's turned on its head in New York City

MARIO TAMA/GETTY

KEEP SCORE!

3min 10sec

Answers
on page 126

Getting a Leg Up

For these lovely lasses, it's sync or swim at London's Trafalgar Square

DANIEL BEREHULAK/GETTY

A
–
B
–
C
–
D
–
E

1 | 2 | 3 | 4 | 5

7
changes

⧗
2min 30sec

Answers
on page 127

KEEP SCORE ★ ❏ ❏ ❏ ❏ ❏ ❏ ❏

Here's Some Moore

A Henry Moore sculpture revamps the scene at Kew Gardens in England

A
—
B
—
C
—
D
—
E

1   2   3   4   5

10 changes

⧗
3min 15sec

Answers
on page 127

KEEP SCORE ★ ❏ ❏ ❏ ❏ ❏ ❏ ❏ ❏ ❏ ❏

Isn't It Good?

This harbor is full of boats made from Norwegian wood

A
—
B
—
C
—
D
—
E

1   2   3   4   5

8
changes

⏳
2min 40sec

Answers
on page 127

KEEP SCORE ★ ❑ ❑ ❑ ❑ ❑ ❑ ❑ ❑

Pumpkin Pilot

Behold, Germany's giddy goddess of gourds

THEO HEIMANN/AFP/GETTY

A

—

B

—

C

—

D

—

E

1 | 2 | 3 | 4 | 5

13
changes

⧗

3min 25sec

Answers
on page 127

KEEP SCORE ★ ❏ ❏ ❏ ❏ ❏ ❏ ❏ ❏ ❏ ❏ ❏ ❏ ❏

Ribbit

Dutch drivers will brake for giant frogs. Wouldn't you?

A
—
B
—
C
—
D
—
E

1 | 2 | 3 | 4 | 5

7
changes

⧗
2min 40sec

Answers
on page 127

KEEP SCORE ★ ❏ ❏ ❏ ❏ ❏ ❏ ❏

Pageantry in Prague

Find the differences among these Czechs, mate

A
–
B
–
C
–
D
–
E

1 | 2 | 3 | 4 | 5

9
changes

⏳
3min 50sec

Answers
on page 127

Not So Grimm

You never know what will show up in this beautiful Black Forest backdrop

DAVE G. HOUSER/CORBIS

A
—
B
—
C
—
D
—
E

1   2   3   4   5

8 changes

⧗

2min 55sec

Answers on page 127

KEEP SCORE ★ ❏ ❏ ❏ ❏ ❏ ❏ ❏ ❏

Puppy!

Well, no, my dear, things have changed

A
–
B
–
C
–
D
–
E

1 | 2 | 3 | 4 | 5

8
changes

⏳
2min 40sec

Answers
on page 127

KEEP SCORE ★ ❏ ❏ ❏ ❏ ❏ ❏ ❏ ❏

Up, Up, and Away

Here's how the Swiss lift off

SANDRO VANNINI/CORBIS

9
changes

KEEP
SCORE!

❏ ❏ ❏ ❏ ❏ ❏ ❏ ❏ ❏

⏳
3min 10sec

Answers
on page 128

Spanish Panache

In Barcelona, we made some un-Gaudi alterations

KEREN SUGETTY

A

—

B

—

C

—

D

—

E

1 | 2 | 3 | 4 | 5

9
changes

⧖
3min 40sec

Answers
on page 128

KEEP SCORE ★ ❏ ❏ ❏ ❏ ❏ ❏ ❏ ❏ ❏

Slip Slidin' Away

Undergoing a transformation in the Middle East

1

2

3

4

5

6

1min 20sec

Answer
on page 128

MASSIMO BORCHI/ CORBIS

One Wired Pachyderm

In Sydney, a post-modern elephant you'll never forget

1

2

3

4

5

6
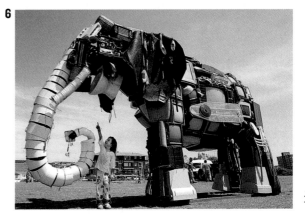

TORSTEN BLACKWOOD/AFP/GETTY

1min 35sec

Answer
on page 128

A Paddle Puzzle

Kayakers at Lake Tahoe face fluctuating conditions

CHRISTINA LEASE/GETTY

A
B
C
D
E

1   2   3   4   5

9
changes

⧗
2min 20sec

Answers
on page 128

KEEP SCORE ★ ❏ ❏ ❏ ❏ ❏ ❏ ❏ ❏ ❏

Equine Elegance

These horses in Prague are dressed to impress

A

B

C

D

E

1 | 2 | 3 | 4 | 5

11
changes

⧖
4min 10sec

Answers
on page 128

KEEP SCORE ★ ❑ ❑ ❑ ❑ ❑ ❑ ❑ ❑ ❑ ❑ ❑

Mickey Slept Here

Take a peek through this mousehole at the Magic Kingdom

A
—
B
—
C
—
D
—
E

1 | 2 | 3 | 4 | 5

10
changes

⧗

3min 30sec

Answers
on page 128

KEEP SCORE ★ ❏ ❏ ❏ ❏ ❏ ❏ ❏ ❏ ❏ ❏

Perplexing Pastoral

There are subtle secrets hidden here in Wales

A

—

B

—

C

—

D

—

E

1 | 2 | 3 | 4 | 5

12
changes

⧖
4min 20sec

Answers
on page 128

KEEP SCORE ★ ❑ ❑ ❑ ❑ ❑ ❑ ❑ ❑ ❑ ❑ ❑ ❑

Arms Up

It's high time to transform Tibet

A
—
B
—
C
—
D
—
E

1   2   3   4   5

9
changes

⏳
3min 40sec

Answers
on page 128

KEEP SCORE ★ ❏ ❏ ❏ ❏ ❏ ❏ ❏ ❏ ❏

Bird's Eye View

What's old is new when you stroll down this Czech street

JON ARNOLD/GETTY

5 | 4 | 3 | 2 | 1

10
changes

KEEP
SCORE!

❏
❏
❏
❏
❏
❏
❏
❏
❏
❏

⧗

4min 30sec

Answers
on page 128

A | B | C | D | E

EXPERT

[Only serious
puzzlers dare to
tread past this
point. Who's in?]

Aspiring Spires

In Red Square, everything is on the up and up

HARALD SUND/GETTY

9
changes

KEEP
SCORE

4min 25sec

Answers
on page 129

Whoa!

Looks like they'll be changing this guard at Buckingham Palace

JIM WATSON/EPA/CORBIS

A
—
B
—
C
—
D
—
E

1　　　2　　　3　　　4　　　5

9
changes

⧗
3min 15sec

Answers
on page 129

KEEP SCORE ★ ❏ ❏ ❏ ❏ ❏ ❏ ❏ ❏ ❏

London Calling

And a daredevil has answered

A
—
B
—
C
—
D
—
E

1   2   3   4   5

9
changes

⧖

3min 35sec

Answers
on page 129

KEEP SCORE ★ ❏ ❏ ❏ ❏ ❏ ❏ ❏ ❏ ❏

Kayak Attack

What would Mark Twain make of this scene?

GABRIEL BUOYS/GETTY

A
—
B
—
C
—
D
—
E

1   2   3   4   5

10
changes

⧗

3min 55sec

Answers
on page 129

KEEP SCORE ★ ▢ ▢ ▢ ▢ ▢ ▢ ▢ ▢ ▢ ▢

In Gay Paree

On a midsummer afternoon, everyone's ready for a cool drink

BRUNO DE HOGUES/GETTY

EXPERT

A

B

C

D

E

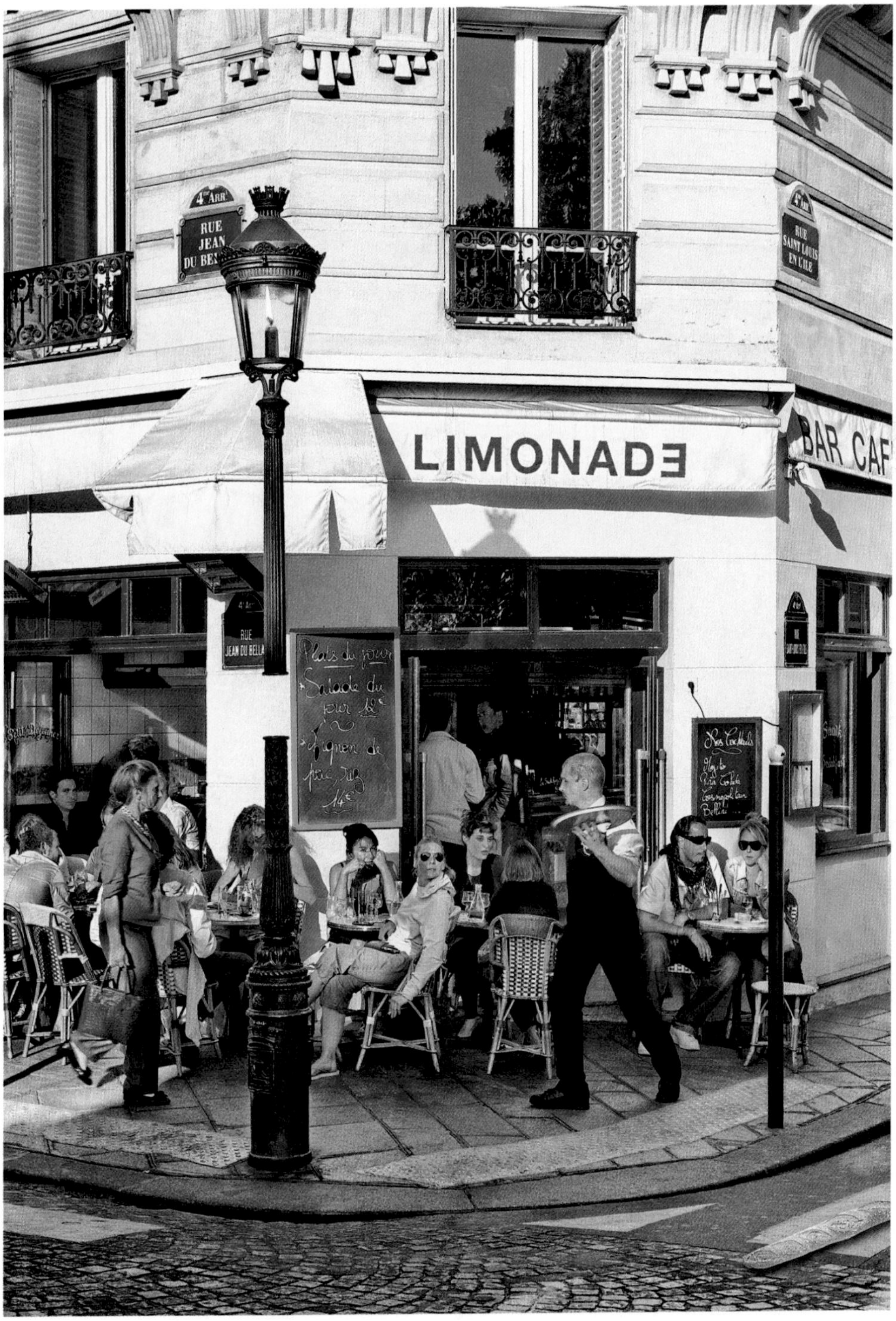

1 | 2 | 3 | 4 | 5

10 changes

KEEP SCORE!

❑
❑
❑
❑
❑
❑
❑
❑
❑
❑

3min 40sec

Answers on page 129

When in Venice . . .

. . . watch out for rising waters

MICHELE CROSERA/REUTERS/CORBIS

A

B

C

D

E

1   2   3   4   5

12
changes

⧗
4min 30sec

Answers
on page 129

KEEP SCORE ★ ❏ ❏ ❏ ❏ ❏ ❏ ❏ ❏ ❏ ❏ ❏ ❏

Morning Recess

Mind the madness among these Madrilenians

LLUIS GENE/AFP/GETTY

A
B
C
D
E

1   2   3   4   5

8
changes

⧖
3min 40sec

Answers
on page 129

KEEP SCORE ★ ❑ ❑ ❑ ❑ ❑ ❑ ❑ ❑

It Doesn't Quite Fit

In the Philippines, an Imelda reject (the only one)

1

2

3

4

5

6

1min 20sec

Answer
on page 129

ROMEO RANOCO/REUTERS/CORBIS

Savory Skewers

Which one of these cooks is less prepared to take your order?

1

2

3

4

5

JAMES BURROWS

6

1min 15sec

Answer
on page 129

GENIUS

[
Finding a single difference
in these puzzles is a
challenge. Finding them all
might be impossible.
]

O Canada

The Calgary Stampede Marching Band goes through a shifty town

GEORGE ROSE/GETTY

A

B

C

D

E

1   2   3   4   5

18
CHANGES

KEEP
SCORE!

⌐ ⌐ ⌐ ⌐ ⌐ ⌐ ⌐ ⌐ ⌐ ⌐ ⌐ ⌐ ⌐ ⌐ ⌐ ⌐ ⌐ ⌐

⌛
5min 50sec

Answers
on page 130

The Fruity Nile

Someone's doling out fun in the sun in Egypt

A
—
B
—
C
—
D
—
E

1   2   3   4   5

13
changes

⧗

4min 40sec

Answers
on page 130

KEEP SCORE ★ ❑ ❑ ❑ ❑ ❑ ❑ ❑ ❑ ❑ ❑ ❑ ❑ ❑

A Dab of India Ink

Final touches sometimes change everything

STRDEL/AFP/GETTY

5

4

3

2

1

A

B

C

D

E

7min 50sec

Answers
on page 130

Let the Good Times Roll

It looks like this party is getting ready to take off

DAVID MCNEW/GETTY

A

B

C

D

E

1   2   3   4   5

18
changes

⏳
6min 10sec

Answers
on page 130

KEEP SCORE ★ ⌐⌐⌐⌐⌐⌐⌐⌐⌐⌐⌐⌐⌐⌐⌐⌐⌐

Bali High

Reach out and touch someone

A

B

C

D

E

1 2 3 4 5

14
changes

⧗
5min 20sec

Answers
on page 130

KEEP SCORE ★ ❏ ❏ ❏ ❏ ❏ ❏ ❏ ❏ ❏ ❏ ❏ ❏ ❏ ❏

You've Got Lemons . . .

. . . Make lemonade! Then solve this puzzle

ERIC GAILLARD/REUTERS/CORBIS

A

B

C

D

E

1   2   3   4   5

11
changes

⏳

5min 20sec

Answers
on page 130

KEEP SCORE ★ ❏ ❏ ❏ ❏ ❏ ❏ ❏ ❏ ❏ ❏ ❏

To Kingdom, Come!

Mickey, Minnie, and friends are waiting

KELLY-MOONEY/CORBIS

A

B

15
CHANGES

KEEP
SCORE!

❏ ❏
❏ ❏
❏ ❏
❏ ❏
❏ ❏
❏ ❏
❏ ❏
❏
❏
❏
❏
❏

C

⧗

5min 40sec

Answers
on page 131

D

E

1   2   3   4   5

Water Taxis

Something's awry on this Venetian canal

1

2

3

4

5

6

3min 20sec

Answer
on page 131

STEFANO AMANTINI/CORBIS

String Theory

It might take a particle physicist to reassemble this colorful quartet

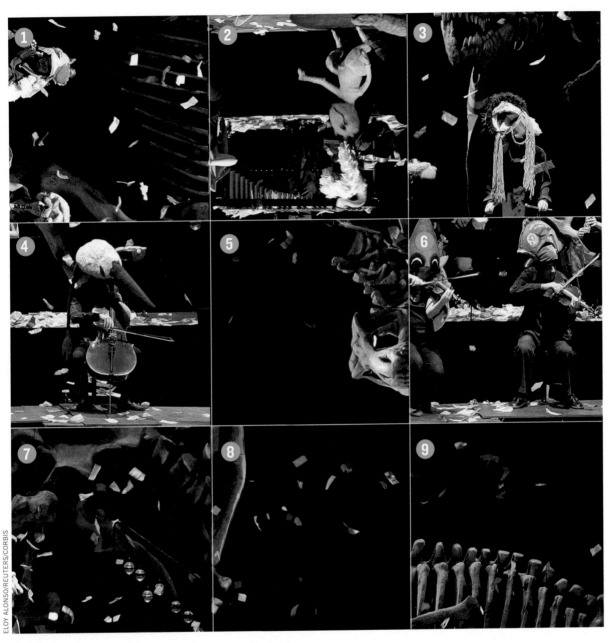

ELOY ALONSO/REUTERS/CORBIS

5min 20sec

Answer
on page 131

KEEP SCORE!

LIFE
CLASSICS

[These puzzles were
specially created with
memorable photos
from the LIFE archives.]

A Man, a Plan, a Canal

But we're in Italy, not Panama

DMITRI KESSEL

6 changes

KEEP SCORE

3min 10sec

Answers on page 131

Foxy Business

Once they've got the scent, these hounds will follow
the hunt through hill, dale, and even town

LARRY BURROWS

A

B

C

D

E

1   2   3   4   5

8
changes

KEEP
SCORE!

❏
❏
❏
❏
❏
❏
❏
❏

⏳

3min 30sec

Answers
on page 131

A Parisian Poseur

This Connecticut Yankee is spinning around
the City of Light and generally having the time of his life

GORDON PARKS

A
–
B
–
C
–
D
–
E

1   2   3   4   5

7
changes

⧗
3min 35sec

Answers
on page 131

KEEP SCORE ★ ❑ ❑ ❑ ❑ ❑ ❑ ❑

To the Manor Born

His is a noble steed indeed

MARK KAUFFMAN

A
–
B
–
C
–
D
–
E

1   2   3   4   5

6
changes

⧗
3min 5sec

Answers
on page 131

Ain't It Grand!

Sure is, but watch out—the first step is a doozy

FRANK SCHERSCHEL

A

B

C

D

E

1   2   3   4   5

7
changes

⧗
3min 40sec

Answers
on page 131

KEEP SCORE ★ ❏ ❏ ❏ ❏ ❏ ❏ ❏

[ANSWERS]
Finished already? Let's see how you did.

[INTRODUCTION]

Page 9: **Trading Places** No. 1 (A2): Palm fronds gently peer down from above. No. 2 (A3): A pigeon confidently glides in for a landing. No. 3 (A4): It's as if that window had never existed. No. 4 (C2): This blanket is a lowrider. No. 5 (C4 to D4): The yellow canopy has lost half its support. No. 6 (C4): The hat is at least a quart too large. No. 7 (D3): She's going to be quite upset when she discovers her earring is missing. No. 8 (D4): Will you accept some pink blankets in lieu of the blue ones? No. 9 (D5): Her braid has gone through an amazing color transformation.

[NOVICE]

Page 11: **Like Clockwork** In No. 3, 10 is the new 12.

Page 12: **Way Beyond Frosty** No. 1 (A4): The temperature must be rising because this chimney melted! No. 2 (B1): One tree less. No. 3 (B3): This time a whole building melted. No. 4 (B4 to C4): She just pulled a 180. No. 5 (C3): This child's hat has gone blue with the cold. No. 6 (C3 to D3): His hat no longer matches his friend's. No. 7 (D3): That boy's yellow stripe turned white. No. 8 (D4): Where'd his leg go?

Page 14: **Totally Digging Colorado** No. 1 (C1): Hello feline friend. No. 2 (C2): He looks better in pants. No. 3 (C2 to D2): Blue like the sky. No. 4 (D4): Buckets of fun. No. 5 (D1): Where did my spray bottle go? Someone got thirsty. No. 6 (E2): A bigger pad for production! No. 7 (E3 to E4): Whatever did happen to Jimmy Hoffa?

Page 16: **Pegasus** No. 1 (A3): Hey, you, get off of my cloud! No. 2 (A3 to B3): My, what big ears you have. No. 3 (B2): This bar better not fade away. No. 4 (D1): The race isn't over until the last song is sung. No. 5 (D2): You put your hind leg in and then you shake it all about. No. 6 (D3): The white stripes ganged up to rub out the black stripe. No. 7 (D4 to E4): A lot of bolts have . . . bolted. No. 8 (E1 to E2): New panelling has been installed along the fence.

Page 18: **Frozen Dinner** In No. 4, a candle has disappeared.

Page 19: **Midday March** In No. 4, a member of the cavalcade has changed her skirt.

Page 20: **Rolling Along** No. 1 (A3): A palm has flipped its top. No. 2 (A4): West Coast sunshine can make just about anything grow faster—including a gangly old palm. No. 3 (C1): It's sure a nice day for boating, isn't it? No. 4 (C3): Every year on this day, she visits California just to stand at the water's edge and contemplate the sea. No. 5 (C4): Okay, who stole the electrical cabinet? No. 6 (C5): She donned a new T-shirt while you weren't looking. No. 7 (D1 to D2): A vampire casts no shadow.

Page 22: **Busman's Holiday** No. 1 (A2 to A3): Someone's getting ready for lunch. No. 2 (A3): He can't hide behind those sunglasses. No. 3 (B5): We've got a really, really big window for you. No. 4 (C1): The wheel is one bolt shy. No. 5 (C3): When did they convert the bus to all electric and ditch the gas tank? Nos. 6 and 7 (C4): The tiger glances backwards only to discover that he's one stripe down. No. 8 (D3 to E5): You remember the old joke, don't you? A tiger walks wherever he wants to.

Page 24: **Dutch Treat** No. 1 (A2): Whoever installed the new windmill vane really goofed. Just wait till it starts turning. No. 2 (A3 to B5): Leaf peeper alert: Autumn's on its way. No. 3 (C3 to C4): That barge is drifting down the canal. No. 4 (C5): The gate arm has totally grown. No. 5 (D4): Are you sure there was a bridge here before? No. 6 (D5): Someone must have had a lot of surplus blue paint. No. 7 (E2 to E3): How do you get more space? Land fill.

Page 26: **Dracula Slept Here** No. 1 (A2): An arborist at work. No. 2 (B2 to C2): Some structural engineering. No. 3 (B3 to C3): Movable towers. No. 4 (B4): No need for an antenna in the digital age. No. 5 (C4): A little window remodel. The count's letting more light in. No. 6 (C4 to D4): Another case of the walking window. No. 7 (D3): Wasn't there a window there?

Page 28: **Do You Buy?** No. 1 (A1): More balls on the lamp for better light. No. 2 (A5): What missing beams? No. 3 (A5 to B5): Not much of a view. No. 4 (B3): Where did the sky walk go? No. 5 (B4): There's no need for a deck in this heat. No. 6 (D5): Bollard moved for a safer day. No. 7 (E1): What a beautiful lamp.

Page 30: **Buzz Off** No. 1 (A4): Where did that bar come from? No. 2 (A2 to B2): Flying high. No. 3 (B4): Bar none. No. 4 (D1): Do I look good in pink? No. 5 (D1): Where'd he go? That insect got hungry. No. 6 (D4): Ships do add to the seascape. No. 7 (E5): Castle in the sand.

Page 32: **Head Over Heels** No. 1 (A4): Who's got short legs? She's got short legs. No. 2 (B1): The building has a bad case of the stripes. No. 3 (B2 to B3): The ferris wheel wants to be center stage. No. 4 (B3): Call the rescue squad. We're one cab down. No. 5 (D1): Rubber duckie, I love you. No. 6 (E1): For want of a nail, a puzzle was made. No. 7 (E2 to E3): Freddy the seal casts a long shadow. No. 8 (E5): The boards had an urge to merge.

Page 34: **Baaaah!** No. 1 (A3): This cap is coming down with the spots. No. 2 (A4): The NO FARTHER sign has moved further. Nos. 3 and 4 (B2): One girl's pendant has snapped its cord, while the other girl looks like she's holding her hands. No. 5 (B2 to C3): She's wearing a matching outfit. No. 6 (B3): Her hat is off-label. No. 7 (C4): This stall is getting more than a bit board. No. 8 (D2): There are no tags on this sheep!

Page 36: **The Sky's the Limit** No. 1 (A5): Another aerial view. No. 2 (C2): The letters took off before this missile. No. 3 (C4 to D4): A growth spurt. No. 4 (E1): Did you know we had a base in New Mexico? No. 5 (E2): Someone scrapped that sign. No. 6 (E3): This missile woke up feeling blue.

Page 38: **Where's Santa?** No. 1 (A2): The antler has lost a branch. No. 2 (A5 to B5): Maybe Santa plans to radio in. No. 3 (B2): This guy gave up on Santa. No. 4 (B3): Green is more festive. No. 5 (D4): Her dress is missing some color.

Page 40: **Making Merry** No. 1 (A4): The cap is waving its tentacles. No. 2 (A5): It's a tall red stripe for a tall multicolored clown. Nos. 3 and 4 (B3): He's whistle-less and she's lost her hair thingie. No. 5 (C1 to D1): The balloon is a little blue. No. 6 (C3): No princesses here. No. 7 (C5 to D5): His costume leg flare is widening out. No. 8 (D1): The stuffed bunny is looking agog and wide-eyed at the goings on.

Page 42: **Chillin' in Southern California** No. 1 (A3 to A5): The southern lights keep shifting around, even at a zoo. No. 2 (B5): Alert, alert! There's an interloper on the ice. No. 3 (C3): Without a label, her yellow overalls just aren't designer clothes. No. 4 (C4): This guy looks like he's blushing. No. 5 (C5): He flaps for fish. No. 6 (D3): Two fish are showing off their tails.

Page 44: **Olé** No. 1 (A3): There's a new balcony for the ring. No. 2 (B2): The sky's the limit for this scaffolding. No. 3 (B2 to C2): Let the sunshine in. No. 4 (B3): From apples to grapes. No. 5 (C5): An unsturdy light. No. 6 (E1): The metal plate is longer.

[MASTER]

7	5	1	6
8	3	2	4

Page 47:
Mirror Image

Page 48: Getting a Leg Up No. 1 (A4 to C4): The Leaning Tower of Pisa is in Italy . . . or is it? No. 2 (B1 to B2): Someone stole the flag poles. Maybe they're not very patriotic in the U.K. No. 3 (C4): Three's company. No. 4 (C5): Some of those Brits are patriotic, after all! No. 5 (D4): It looks like these swimmers have some competition. No. 6 (D5 to E5): Here's hoping that swimmer didn't drown. No. 7 (E2): She doesn't know her right from her left.

Page 50: Here's Some Moore No. 1 (A1): That's one tall tree. No. 2 (A2): What goes up must come down. No. 3 (A4): That tree was eating up too much oxygen. No. 4 (B1): Do sculptures grow? No. 5 (B2): Things are on the up and up and up and up. Nos. 6 and 7 (C3): Protect from all elements . . . or not, and could the hat be possessed? It's starting to glow. No. 8 (C4 to C5): That crate's been reinforced. No. 9 (D1): Pastel colors are his thing. No. 10 (E5): This wooden leg got lonely and joined its friends.

Page 52: Isn't It Good? No. 1 (A3): The sky is a lot more colorful all of a sudden. No. 2 (A4 to A5): Mountain climbers rejoice! Here's one you haven't climbed before. No. 3 (B3): This barn door is no more. No. 4 (B5 to C5): Now this house matches the water. No. 5 (C4): The harbor view has improved. No. 6 (D1): What a fortuitous name for a boat. No. 7 (D4): The seagull has perfect balance on top of its new buoy. No. 8 (E2): The ship's label must have gone swimming.

Page 54: Pumpkin Pilot No. 1 (A1 to A2): The shelf is a bit smaller now. No. 2 (A2): Big onions mean big tears. Nos. 3 and 4 (A3): Not only is the steering wheel singing "Let's get together and be one board," it's also casting a deeper shadow. No. 5 (A4): She's got one tall seat back. No. 6. (B1): The . . . er, headlight must have fallen off. No. 7 (B2): Now the gourds wrap around the smokestack. No. 8 (C3): Who replaced the yellow squash with a green one? No. 9 (C3 to C4): I don't know about you but we find this pumpkin more than a little ominous. No. 10 (D5): One of these pumpkins has lost its stem. Nos. 11 and 12 (E1): The cat is stalking the mouse, but clever mouse knew what was good for it and skedaddled. No. 13 (E5): Of course, the dog chases the cat.

Page 56: Ribbit No. 1 (A5): The right eye must see well enough to make up for the missing left one. No. 2 (B3 to B4): The frog wasn't in the mood to wear its letters today. No. 3 (C4): According to the new sign, horses might be joining the traffic jam. No. 4 (D2 to D3): The white gate is learning to hop like a frog. No. 5 (D5): The road marker is playing peekaboo. No. 6 (E4): Two lanes turn into one. No. 7 (E5): The frog got lost, looking for its princess.

Page 58: Pageantry in Prague No. 1 (A4): His hat is brim-full. No. 2 (A5): This horn is solid, man. No. 3 (B3): They must call this horse Spotty. No. 4 (B4): Quick, get the sewing kit. His uniform has popped a button. No. 5 (B4 to C4): He blows so well, they've given him a medal. No. 6 (C2): His medal is starting to turn green. No. 7 (D1): He's pulled on his high boot. No. 8 (D2 to E3): The saddle blanket is almost solid red now. No. 9 (E4): The horse's button was sold to the silversmith for beer money.

.

Page 60: Not So Grimm No. 1 (B3): Another chimney for those chilly mornings. Nos. 2 and 3 (B4): The attic wall has changed color, and there is one window less. No. 4 (C1): These vacationers must be hitching a ride home, because someone drove off with their camper. No. 5 (C5): It's sink or swim for that patch of grass. No. 6 (D4 to D5): This canoe is pea green with envy. No. 7 (E1): Quack, quack! No. 8 (E2 to E3): Did that duck get hungry and eat the paddle for dinner?

Page 62: Puppy! No. 1 (A5): In case you were thinking of lighting up, think again! No. 2 (B2): His tusk is trying to shake her hand. Nos. 3 and 4 (C5): Maybe someone's making a wish with his missing rib bone, and he may be old but he still has incredible balance, even without his femur. Nos. 5 and 6 (D2): She's training to be an air traffic director, and it's time to put away your camera phone. No. 7 (D3): A clown dropped in to brighten the day. No. 8 (E1): Rapunzel, Rapunzel, let down your long hair!

Page 64: Up, Up, and Away! No. 1 (A1): This balloon is westbound. No. 2 (B3): One of these letters is not like the others. No. 3 (C1): One balloon is awfully musical. Nos. 4 and 5 (C3): A balloon has gone wireless and lost its basket. Watch out! No. 6 (D2 to E2): This balloon park is shack-a-licious! No. 7 (D3): Up, up, and upside down! No. 8 (E1): She can't make up her mind which way to look. No. 9 (E4 to E5): Nothing can replace the mother-daughter bond.

Page 66: Spanish Panache No. 1 (A2 to A3): The crane is playing tricks on us. No. 2 (A4): A tree grows in Barcelona. No. 3 (A5): Barcelona is so eco-friendly, this tower is going green! No. 4 (B2): The house has taken a decidedly asymmetrical turn. No. 5 (B4 to C4): My, what big circles you have! No. 6 (B5): Did anyone see who used white-out on these tiles? No. 7 (C3): Can you say "pest control"? No. 8 (E2): Whoever took the red and black tile felt bad and put it back. No. 9 (E5): These tiles are not dependable. They keep changing their colors!

Page 68: Slip Slidin' Away Part of this palm tree is missing in photo No. 1. Did it decide to go for a ride before the crowds arrive?

Page 69: One Wired Pachyderm In photo No. 5, the man's new shirt goes perfectly with the elephant's recycled parts.

Page 70: A Paddle Puzzle No. 1 (A5): I can see clearly now, the cloud has gone . . . No. 2 (B1 to C1): There are a lot of boats on the water today. Be careful! No. 3 (B2): Wig time! No. 4 (B3): That's one long kayak! No. 5 (B4): Canopies look better in red. No. 6 (C1): Attack of the orange kayaks! No. 7 (C3): It's this way, honey. No, it's that way. No. 8 (C4): Who wants duck for dinner? No. 9 (C5): Six is an unlucky number, anyway!

Page 72: Equine Elegance No. 1 (A1): Somehow a rider broke off the tip of his flagpole. No. 2 (A2 to B2): This flag has gone crimson. No. 3 (A5): Big-eared horses hear their riders' commands better, at least

that's the theory. Nos. 4 and 5 (B2): As the lamp pole shot up seemingly overnight, the tower disappeared. No. 6 (B3): He's shy an ear. No. 7 (D1): This leg is just too much of a good thing. Nos. 8 and 9 (D3): A horse is no longer lifting his leg, and a cross has fallen off a blanket. No. 10 (E2): Walking without a hoof has got to be painful. No. 11 (E3 to E4): Who washed the saddle blanket in hot water? It wasn't shrink-free. But now it is.

Page 74: Mickey Slept Here No. 1 (A3 to B3): The electricians installed an extra overhead. No. 2 (B2 to C2): The wallpaper is double curvy here. No. 3 (C2): Mickey likes a very tall glass of water at bedtime. No. 4 (C3): No, Mickey, pink trim is actually quite masculine. No. 5 (D1): To the unknown person who took the drawer knob: if you return it, there will be no questions asked. No. 6 (D2): Mickey lost a star, or at least his shoe did. No. 7 (D3): Really, having your initial on a bed is a little ostentatious. No. 8 (E1): This just became one very long floorboard. No. 9 (E2 to E3): The way it's going, eventually the rug will be spotless. No. 10 (E5): The armoire's side panel now reaches the ground.

Page 76: Perplexing Pastoral No. 1 (A2): Welsh chimney sweeps are known for stretching their chimneys as they clean them. No. 2 (B2 to B3): Pink shutters are all the rage now. No. 3 (B3): The window is trying to match the chimney in height. No. 4 (B4): The building gained a spiral. No. 5 (B5): Where did this gargoyle come from? No. 6 (C5): Okay, now pay attention. The painting hanging inside the window had a slice taken out of it. No. 7 (D2): Two tulips volunteered for extra duty. No. 8 (D4): The arrows can't make up their minds. Nos. 9 and 10 (D5): Not only did the building lose a window, the garden statue has left the premises. No. 11 (E2): The planter now has more room to plant plants, like those two tulips above. No. 12 (E2 to E3): The shadow has been smoothed out.

Page 78: Arms Up No. 1 (A2): In Tibet, gold grows from building tops. No. 2 (A3): This flag wants to stand out from the rest. No. 3 (B1): A room with no view times two. No. 4 (B2): Things are getting a little swirly-whirly around here. No. 5 (B3): The bottom half of this building wanted to be like its top. No. 6 (B5): Good luck getting up these stairs! No. 7 (B5): It must be Valentine's Day. No. 8 (D4): Her waist tie is flying higher. No. 9 (D5): It's hip to be a purple square . . . or rectangle.

Page 80: Bird's Eye View No. 1 (A2): The yellow wall has a new paint job. No. 2 (A3): An enterprising home-owner has added a new skylight. No. 3 (A3 to B3): This skylight has restless window syndrome. No. 4 (A4):

Chimney Whimney had a great fall . . . No. 5 (B2 to C2): The roof is a bit edgier today. No. 6 (B4): The attic window has been bricked in. No. 7 (C2): Two windows have joined forces as one. No. 8 (D5): He's just walking along, walking along. No. 9 (E2): The sunlight is bleaching this umbrella away. No. 10 (E3): The plaza tiles have been filled in.

[EXPERT]

Page 83: **Aspiring Spires** No. 1 (A2): An easterly breeze. No. 2 (A5): Scramble the fighters! No. 3 (A5): They keep building them higher and higher. No. 4 (B1): Time flies when you're having fun with LIFE Picture Puzzles! No. 5 (B3 to C3): Colors of the rainbow. No. 6 (B4): Another minaret. No. 7 (C1): No more window. No. 8 (D2 to E2): Steeple, goodbye! No. 9 (E2): Be green.

Page 84: **Whoa!** No. 1 (A1 to B1): Having an off day. No. 2 (A4): Another pillar for good measure. No. 3 (A5): Darker nights. No. 4 (B4): Pigeon galore. No. 5 (C4): Now he's on the blue team. No. 6 (C5): Are all the guards ambidextrous or just this one? No. 7 (D1): Don't place a bet on this three-legged horse. No. 8 (D2): This horse was tired of wearing all black. No. 9 (D5): A lawsuit waiting to happen.

Page 86: **London Calling** No. 1 (A5): Werewolves beware when there is a full moon above. No. 2 (B1): A little more gold, please. No. 3 (B3): We thought it was taller. No. 4 (B4): The law of gravity is not in this cyclist's favor. No. 5 (C5): Where did my spire go? No. 6 (D1 to E2): Sometimes less is more. No. 7 (D3): There's a problem with the structural integrity. No. 8 (D4): Adding some light to a dark place. No. 9 (D5 to E5): Is someone expecting a baby girl?

Page 88: **Kayak Attack** No. 1 (A4 to A5): No more mesh. Nos. 2 and 3 (B1): A Union Jack, plus the tallest palm tree I've ever seen! No. 4 (B2): Two of these poles were fighting so a third one stepped in to break it up. No. 5 (B3 to C3): There were too many windows. No. 6 (D1): Beware of the vanishing kayakers. No. 7 (D4 to D5): They call me mellow yellow. Quite rightly! No. 8 (E1 to E2): This buoy is making a quick getaway. No. 9 (E3): Jaws! No. 10 (E5): Bananarama!

Page 90: **In Gay Paree** No. 1 (A2): The building has some buckteeth. No. 2 (A5 to B5): The two small blocks joined into one. No. 3 (B1): Hopefully those missing letters didn't fall on someone's head. No. 4 (B2): Candles give such a nice light. No. 5 (B4): This *E* is not making it easy. No. 6 (C1): One more support to hold up the façade. No. 7 (C2): Paris is known for its hovering lampposts. No. 8 (D1): This café needed some greenery. No. 9 (D5): Now this pole is as tall as the waiter. No. 10 (E5): It's a French thing.

Page 92: **When in Venice . . .** No. 1 (A1): You can never have too many statues. No. 2 (A2 to B2): Double trouble. No. 3 (A4): These are old buildings, sometimes small pillars fall off. Nos. 4 and 5 (B2 to C2): Taller + bluer = flaggier. No. 6 (B3): Reach for the stars! Scaffolding! No. 5 (B5): The builders forgot one. Nos. 8 and 9 (C3): A more contemporary window design and another steeple don't hurt the landscape one bit. No. 10 (C4): Watch out for the missing balcony. No. 11 (C4 to D4): Either this girl only has one arm, or we just can't see it. No. 12 (D4): A nonthreatening police officer.

Page 94: **Morning Recess** No. 1 (A1): The crane is no more. No. 2 (B3): Velazquez has a big head . . . and maybe a perm! No. 3 (C4): The decal has disappeared. No. 4 (D2): His shirt is moody. No. 5 (D2): While the kids were playing tag, this curtain crept down. No. 6 (D3): This Harry Potter protégé made himself invisible. No. 7 (D5): This way and that way. No. 8 (E5): Put your shoes on, kid!

Page 96: **It Doesn't Quite Fit** In photo No. 6, the passenger has no passenger handle to hold onto.

Page 97: **Savory Skewers** You may have a hard time figuring out the cook's name in photo No. 3. His name tag's missing.

Page 99: O Canada No. 1 (A3 to B3): The mountain appears to be pumping itself up. No. 2 (B3): As the mountain goes up, the roof goes down. No. 3 (B4): A street lamp has blown away. Nos. 4 and 5 (B5): As the rubberized lamp stretched out, a tree moved into the neighborhood. Nos. 6, 7 and 8 (C3): A window fled as the siren and street light poles both reached for the sky. No. 9 (C4): In a reversal of autumn, the flag's maple leaf has gone from red to green. No. 10 (C5): The light has changed. Of course, it didn't switch positions, but never mind. No. 11 (D1): His pants have lost a loop. No. 12 (D2): Repeated use appears to have misshapen this cymbal. No. 13 (D3): From Yamaha to off-label with one quick clone brush. No. 14 (E2): Never use vanishing cream on your sax. No. 15 (E2): They call him Mr. Long Legs. They just call his shadow, shadow. No. 16 (E3): This shadow's gone to that mystical place in the sky, shadowland. No. 17 (E3 to E4): The manhole doesn't need to be covered anymore—because it ain't there. No. 18 (E4): Watching a parade is a timeless event, at least once your watch has been stolen.

Page 100: The Fruity Nile No. 1 (A1): Demolition. No. 2 (A2): Who's been telling lies to make this building grow like Pinocchio's nose? No. 3 (A5): The high rise decided to get shorty. No. 4 (B2): The horizon will never be the same with that palm tree. No. 5 (B3): No need for the wood support. It's all smooth sailing. No. 6 (B4): Goodbye, banana. No. 7 (C1): Can't get enough of the color blue. No. 8 (C4): Who needs a profile when you've got so many bananas? No. 9 (C5): Turn that floating banana back around. No. 10 (D1): This banana forgot to put its Dole on today. Nos. 11, 12, and 13 (D5): A sandal fell in the water, and the boat has a design complex . . . two of them. Anchors away.

Page 102: A Dab of India Ink No. 1 (A1): There's no symbolism to the missing cymbal. No. 2 (A2 to B2): The painter has changed the background color in one scene. No. 3 (A3): Someone has lost his bird's eye view. No. 4 (A3): The scroll has been widened. No. 5 (A4): He's being examined for the medical condition of flippy legs. Nos. 6 and 7 (A5): Mr. Red and Mr. Green are now Bluemen. No. 8 (A5 to B5): Almost everyone likes yellowtail. No. 9 (B1): When all you do is sit around and meditate, you've got plenty of time for your beard to grow. No. 10 (B2): Apparently, a flower doesn't grow in India. No. 11 (B3 to C3): Someone tugged on this painting once too often and pulled it out of shape. No. 12 (B3 to C4): With a jacket this color, he must be of royal blood. No. 13 (B4 to C5): They're about to discover that, indeed, smoking can be hazardous to your health. No. 14 (C1 to C2): Puss 'n Fish. Puss 'n Fish. No. 15 (C2 to D2): Did you ever read *Painting Through the Looking Glass*? It will flip you out. No. 16 (C4): This guy needs an immediate visit from the Fuller Brush, man. No. 17 (D3 to D4): Now which do you like

better, a green or blue background? No. 18 (D4): And do you like blue or green skies? No. 19 (E2): This plant is leafing out.

Page 104: Let the Good Times Roll No. 1 (A1): When the red kite hawk goes glide-glide-glidin' along . . . No. 2 (A4 to B4): The tower had an upgrade. No. 3 (B3): But the dowel has been downsized. Nos. 4 and 5 (C2): When her bracelet gained a spiral, her other hand disappeared. No. 6 (C3): A different dowel must have fallen off. No. 7 (C3 to D3): Her wing is getting a little ragged. No. 8 (C4): The triangles have resequenced themselves. No. 9 (D1): It was time for a blue spot, wasn't it? No. 10 (D1 to D2): Her earring popped a bead. No. 11 (D4): He's having a kicking good time. No. 12 (E1): She's taking a restroom break. Nos. 13, 14, and 15 (E3): The extra lamp has illuminated the true meaning of LIFE, so let the drumming begin. Nos. 16, 17, and 18 (E5): Is that Woody behind the big-brimmed hat? If so, give him an extra star.

Page 106: Bali High No. 1 (A1 to B1): Didn't you get the blue flag memo? No. 2 (A5 to B5): That memo was followed up with one about a missing flag. No. 3 (B1): A bird carried off one of the sheaves of wheat. Nos. 4 and 5 (B2): We're up one flower and down one decorative wall scroll. Nos. 6 and 7 (B3): Now there's an extra itsy-bitsy window, while the wooden drawer has lost its stone latch. No. 8 (C1): The flagpole is clearly retreating backwards. No. 9 (C2 to C3): Now he's a golden god. Nos. 10 and 11 (C3): After the miracle of the levitating lamp, everyone relaxes with a little game of beach ball. No. 12 (C4): Someone filched her arm band. No. 13 (E1): Now we know where Chuck Berry learned how to duck walk. No. 14 (E3): He had a yellow belly band. Now he has a green one. Will miracles never cease?

Page 108: You've Got Lemons . . . No. 1 (A5): A flag, far, far away. No. 2 (B2): What will they do without their point? No. 3 (B4): A flag by any other color wouldn't blow as sweet. Nos. 4 and 5 (B5): A no-star hotel, that's totally backwards. No. 6 (C3): Another window means fewer lemons, but you probably have enough, anyway. No. 7 (D2): An open door policy. No. 8 (D3): A little jangle is missing from her arm bangle. No. 9 (D4): She's more flexible than Gumby! No. 10 (D5): sssssssssssss-up? No. 11 (E1): A green thumb added more red flowers.

Page 110: To Kingdom, Come! No. 1 (A4 to A5): In the Magic Kingdom, trees leaf out on demand. Or else. No. 2 (B2 to C2): Think pink! No. 3 (B3): They may have to call in Sherlock Holmes to solve the mysterious case of the missing castle window. No. 4 (B4): A new flag flies at the castle. No. 5 (C4): The Wolf must have dropped his cane while chasing Little Red Riding Hood. No. 6 (C5): Her cuff has been blued. No. 7 (D1): He likes to hummy a little tune about his hunny. No. 8 (D2): Tigger is sporting a new belly stripe. No. 9 (D2 to D3): Did you ever notice how big Pluto's eyes are? Nos. 10 and 11 (D3): Minnie's dress may be short one spot but the big news is that Mickey's got a pinkie, Mickey's got a pinkie. No. 12 (D4): And his pants have popped their buttons. Nos. 13 and 14 (E2): My, what big hands you have for a dwarf. And Goofy, what wide pants legs. No. 15 (E3 to E4): They're going to have to change Goofy's name to Gummy.

Page 112: Water Taxis There's a conflicting arrow in photo No. 3.

<table>
<tr><td>5</td><td>9</td><td>8</td></tr>
<tr><td>3</td><td>1</td><td>7</td></tr>
<tr><td></td><td>6</td><td>4</td></tr>
</table>

Page 113:
String Theory
Did any of you geniuses guess that 1, 2, 5, and 8 are flipped?

[LIFE CLASSICS]

Page 115: A Man, a Plan, a Canal
No. 1 (B2): Let there be light! Let there be windows! No. 2 (B4): This doorway makes for a really grand entrance. No. 3 (C2 to C3): We think they call this a long boat. No. 4 (C3): It looks like the gondola's risso sank beneath the waves. No. 5 (C4): We've played a nasty trick on the gondolier and his pole. No. 6 (E1 to E5): If the water keeps rising, everyone's going swimming.

Page 116: Foxy Business No. 1 (A4): A chimney has been swept away. No. 2 (B5): The shingles are steadily marching down the wall. Nos. 3 and 4 (C3): A bystander waits patiently by her car as the Post Office sign drifts slowly downward. No. 5 (D1): Of course you've heard of the invisible man but this is the invisible wheel. Or it would be if the formula worked properly. As it is, it's the half-visible wheel. *Sigh.* No. 6 (D5): The dog trots freely

in the street, at least until the hunt begins in earnest. Nos. 7 and 8 (E2): A brown fetlock may blend in well with the rest of the horse but dyslexic license plates can be quite difficult to read.

Page 118: A Parisian Poseur No. 1 (A1): A tower is missing. What tower? Guess. You're in Paris, after all. No. 2 (B1): The lamp produces so much light, it's floating on air. No. 3 (B3): He may have ditched his glasses but it hasn't helped much. No. 4 (B5 to C5): It's another case of a missing street light. No. 5 (D3): His jacket is going to keep him just a bit warmer now. No. 6 (E3 to E4): We've heard of Big Foot, but this seems to be Big Shoe. No. 7 (E4): The fender has been snipped short.

Page 120: To the Manor Born No. 1 (A4): That disappearing window really has no manners. No. 2 (A5 to B5): More branches provide the hoi polloi with more summer shade. No. 3 (B3): This is what happens when a top hat becomes a stovepipe. No. 4 (E1): Beware of the shrinking waiter. No. 5 (E3): Horsey's trying its very best to curtsey. No. 6 (E5): Poor duckie is a long, long way from Golden Pond.

Page 122: Ain't It Grand! No. 1 (A5): The plane is backtracking. No. 2 (B3): The canyon walls are going through some tectonic uplift. No. 3 (C2): The new hat is just ridiculous on him. No. 4 (D1): One of these shadows has been scrubbed clean. No. 5 (D4): He may have copied his taste in hats from the gentleman next to him, but on him it looks good. No. 6 (E3): He's got longer legs and knockier knees. No. 7 (E5): If the safety rail loses any more bars, it won't be very safe at all.

Old and New

In Egypt, the Sphinx has company

BRUNO MORANDI/GETTY

11
changes

KEEP
SCORE

3min 55sec

A — B — C — D — E

1   2   3   4   5

Can you solve the riddle of the Sphinx?

ANSWERS No. 1 (A1): They're landing in an airplane, don't know when they'll take off again. **No. 2 (A1 to C2):** This sphinx is getting a swollen head. **No. 3 (B1 to C2):** A flock of seagulls, I mean pigeons, is on the prowl. **No. 4 (C3 to D3):** The building has been repaired with cement. **No. 5 (C5):** The siren has been silenced. **No. 6 (D3):** I want my DirecTV, so give me back my trakking satellite dish. **No. 7 (D3 to E3):** Major Squab to ground control: "I'm coming in for a landing." **No. 8 (D3 to D4):** The shutters have been yellowed over time. **Nos. 9 and 10 (D4):** Talk about coincidences! A window and a blue stripe have been eliminated. **No. 11 (E3 to E4):** The pedestal has been stretched.

LIFE THE ESSENTIAL

PICTURE PUZZLE

👉 CAN YOU SPOT THE DIFFERENCES? 👈

THE 11TH BOOK IN THE WILDLY POPULAR SERIES
4 LEVELS: NOVICE · MASTER · EXPERT · GENIUS

WELCOME TO LIFE'S ELEVENTH
PICTURE PUZZLE BOOK

We've been across America and around the world with our Picture Puzzle books. Our spot-the-difference puzzles have celebrated the holidays, gone on vacation, and even gone to the dogs, camels, elephants, giraffes, and polar bears. We've created mystery and whodunit puzzles out of timeless characters, such as Sherlock Holmes and the Thin Man, using photos from classic movies and television series. And it's all been tremendous fun. We've had a wonderful time carefully shaping each puzzle to offer just the right amount of challenge to new puzzlers, while making sure to find a fresh approach for each new book—keeping things lively for our most loyal puzzlers. And we must be doing something right because LIFE's Picture Puzzle books remain the most popular of the genre. Thank you.

This is our eleventh Picture Puzzle book. Hard to believe. With ten under our belt, we looked upon this one as something of a new beginning. As our title indicates, we took it as our mission to focus on the essentials: What is it that makes for the most colorful, most fun, most challenging picture puzzle. What goes into the perfect picture puzzle? We asked our photo editors and our wild-and-crazy Puzzle Master to ask those questions as they approached each page in this book, and we think they've come up with our best collection of puzzles yet. Is the book perfect? Only you can say.

Sticking to the essentials means keeping what works. Our Novice section still offers a gentle introduction for beginning puzzlers. Then we gradually increase the challenge throughout our Master and Expert sections. Think of it as on-the-job training. But a word of warning. By the time you attempt our Genius section, you should be ready to tackle some truly baffling conundrums. Otherwise, we fear these puzzles may master you.

[OUR CUT-UP PUZZLES: EASY AS 1-2-3]

We snipped a photo into four or six pieces. Then we rearranged the pieces and numbered them.

Your mission: Beneath each cut-up puzzle, write the number of the piece in the box where it belongs.

Check the answer key at the back of the book to see what the reassembled image looks like.

[HOW TO PLAY THE PUZZLES]

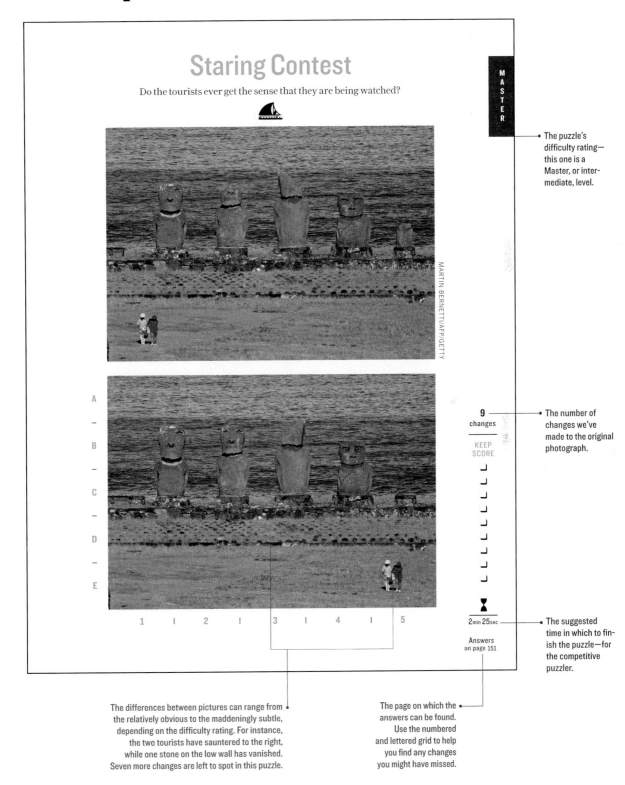

Staring Contest

Do the tourists ever get the sense that they are being watched?

MASTER

MARTIN BERNETTI/AFP/GETTY

The puzzle's difficulty rating—this one is a Master, or intermediate, level.

9 changes

The number of changes we've made to the original photograph.

KEEP SCORE

2min 25sec

The suggested time in which to finish the puzzle—for the competitive puzzler.

Answers on page 151

The differences between pictures can range from the relatively obvious to the maddeningly subtle, depending on the difficulty rating. For instance, the two tourists have sauntered to the right, while one stone on the low wall has vanished. Seven more changes are left to spot in this puzzle.

The page on which the answers can be found. Use the numbered and lettered grid to help you find any changes you might have missed.

NOVICE

[
These puzzles are for everyone:
rookies and veterans,
young and old. Start here, and
sharpen your skills.
]

Remember to Floss

My, what big teeth you have!

EITAN ABRAMOVICH/AFP/GETTY

8
changes

KEEP
SCORE

❑
❑
❑
❑
❑
❑
❑
❑

⏳
2min 10sec

Answers
on page 251

Leap of Faith

The cord won't break. The cord won't break. The cord won't break.

7
changes

KEEP
SCORE

❏
❏
❏
❏
❏
❏
❏

⌛

1min 55sec

Answers
on page 251

Land of the Giants . . .

. . . Or some very tiny horses

CHRISTIAN FISCHER/AFP/GETTY

A
—
B
—
C
—
D
—
E

1   2   3   4   5

9
changes

⧗

2min 40sec

Answers
on page 251

KEEP SCORE ★ ❏ ❏ ❏ ❏ ❏ ❏ ❏ ❏ ❏

You've Heard of the Trojan Horse?

Well, don't trust a wooden elephant, either

A

B

C

D

E

1 | 2 | 3 | 4 | 5

9
changes

⏳
2min 55sec

Answers
on page 251

KEEP SCORE ★ ❏ ❏ ❏ ❏ ❏ ❏ ❏ ❏ ❏

Stairway to Heaven

When it's springtime on China's Great Wall,
everybody feels like getting married

RANDY OLSON/NATIONAL GEOGRAPHIC/GETTY

A — B — C — D — E

1   2   3   4   5

7
changes

⧗
2min 15sec

Answers
on page 251

Tee Time

And they've got caddies that never talk back

1

2

3

4

5

6

0min 30sec

Answer
on page 251

Pass the Hot Sauce

Eats cars for lunch

1

2

3

4

5

6

GREG WOOD/AFP/GETTY

0min 45sec

Answer
on page 251

Crazy, Dude!

The amazing thing is not how well they surf, but that they do surf at all

GABRIEL BOUYS/AFP/GETTY

8
changes

KEEP
SCORE

❑
❑
❑
❑
❑
❑
❑
❑

⌛

2min 15sec

Answers
on page 251

Pumping Canine

How many beagle reps can you do?

JUNKO KIMURA/GETTY

A
—
B
—
C
—
D
—
E

1   2   3   4   5

6
changes

⏳
2min 10sec

Answers
on page 251

KEEP SCORE ★ ❑ ❑ ❑ ❑ ❑ ❑

Circle of Friends

Off we go into the wild blue yonder

A
—
B
—
C
—
D
—
E

1   2   3   4   5

8
changes

⧗
2min 50sec

Answers
on page 251

KEEP SCORE ★ ❏ ❏ ❏ ❏ ❏ ❏ ❏ ❏

Head Over Heels

Or is it really heels over head?

MARCEL ANTONISSE/AFP/GETTY

7
changes

⧗

1min 45sec

Answers
on page 252

A
—
B
—
C
—
D
—
E

1   2   3   4   5

Bumper-to-Bumper Traffic

Let's hope the brakes are working

MICHAEL JOHN O'NEILL/GETTY

A

B

C

D

E

1 2 3 4 5

6
changes

KEEP
SCORE

❏
❏
❏
❏
❏
❏

⏳

2min 55sec

Answers
on page 252

Symmetry in Stone

The rhythm of life is peaceful at the Taj Mahal

FRANS LEMMENS/GETTY

A
—
B
—
C
—
D
—
E

1   2   3   4   5

8
changes

3min 40sec

Answers
on page 252

KEEP SCORE ★ ❏ ❏ ❏ ❏ ❏ ❏ ❏ ❏

Please Don't Feed the Dino

But gentle pats on the head are gratefully accepted

A

—

B

—

C

—

D

—

E

1   2   3   4   5

9
changes

KEEP
SCORE

☐ ☐
☐ ☐
☐ ☐
☐ ☐
☐ ☐
☐ ☐
☐ ☐
☐ ☐
☐

⧗

2min **35**sec

Answers
on page 252

Space Age Dubai

Don't let the angle fool you. We're definitely not in Pisa.

10
changes

KEEP
SCORE

☐
☐
☐
☐
☐
☐
☐
☐
☐
☐

⧗

2min 25sec

Answers
on page 252

Flag Day

Something about the photo looks a little staged

NASA

A
—
B
—
C
—
D
—
E

1 | 2 | 3 | 4 | 5

8
changes

⏳
2min 45sec

Answers
on page 252

KEEP SCORE ★ ❑ ❑ ❑ ❑ ❑ ❑ ❑ ❑

What's Buggin' You?

The pest control guys have their hands full

A

B

C

D

E

1   2   3   4   5

8
changes

⧗
3min 45sec

Answers
on page 252

KEEP SCORE ★ ❑ ❑ ❑ ❑ ❑ ❑ ❑ ❑

Fishy Business

Separate the water and the air before someone gets eaten

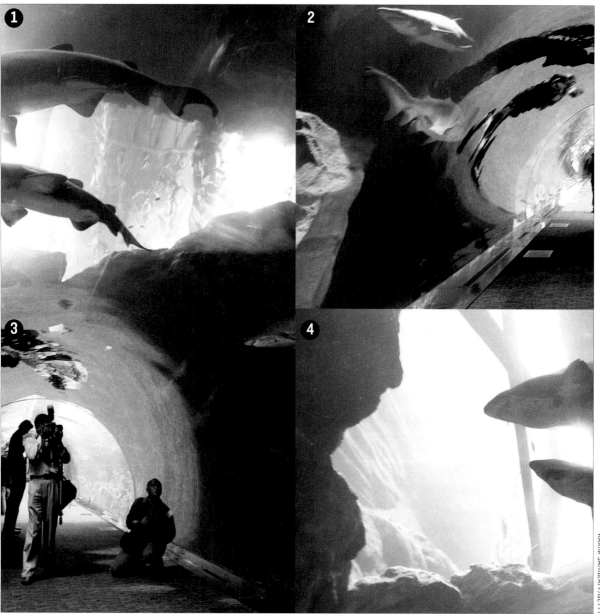

⏳ 0min 30sec

Answer
on page 252

KEEP SCORE

Everything's Coming Up Roses

The Tournament of Roses Parade can be great fun, but stay away from the robot's feet

KEEP SCORE

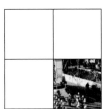

0min 45sec

Answer
on page 252

Balancing Act

It takes steady nerves to ride the slide

A

B

C

D

E

1　　　2　　　3　　　4　　　5

10
changes

⧗
3min 35sec

Answers
on page 252

KEEP SCORE ★ ❏ ❏ ❏ ❏ ❏ ❏ ❏ ❏ ❏ ❏

Nice Kitties, Nice Kitties

Some catnip would come in handy right about now

EYESWIDEOPEN/GETTY

9
changes

KEEP
SCORE

❏ ❏ ❏ ❏ ❏ ❏ ❏ ❏ ❏

⧗
3min 55sec

Answers
on page 253

MASTER

[Here, puzzles get
a little harder. You'll
need to raise
your game a level.]

And the Winner Is . . .

. . . You, by a nose, if you solve this puzzle

FERENC ISZA/AFP/GETTY

A
—
B
—
C
—
D
—
E

1 | 2 | 3 | 4 | 5

10 changes

KEEP SCORE

3min 50sec

Answers on page 253

Cliffhanger

Sometimes you have nowhere to go but up

A

B

C

D

E

1   2   3   4   5

10
changes

KEEP
SCORE

❏
❏
❏
❏
❏
❏
❏
❏
❏
❏

⌛

3min 15sec

Answers
on page 253

A Walk on the Wild Side

It's no place to space out

STOCKTREK IMAGES/GETTY

9
changes

KEEP
SCORE

2min 45sec

Answers
on page 253

5

4

3

2

1

A | B | C | D | E

Hey There, Little Fella

This looks like the beginning of
a beautiful friendship

A
—
B
—
C
—
D
—
E

1   2   3   4   5

10
changes

⧗
3min 20sec

Answers
on page 253

Celestial Season

If it's the spring equinox on the Salisbury Plain,
then these must be Druids

A
—
B
—
C
—
D
—
E

1   2   3   4   5

11
changes

⧗
2min 10sec

Answers
on page 253

Imperial Waters

This lacks only a czar

A

B

C

D

E

1 | 2 | 3 | 4 | 5

12
changes

KEEP
SCORE

❏
❏
❏
❏
❏
❏
❏
❏
❏
❏
❏
❏

⧗

4min 15sec

Answers
on page 253

A Slippery Slope

Getting to the bottom of this puzzle
would be really cool

A
—
B
—
C
—
D
—
E

1   2   3   4   5

9
changes

⏳
3min 10sec

Answers
on page 253

KEEP SCORE ★ ❏ ❏ ❏ ❏ ❏ ❏ ❏ ❏ ❏

Poetry in Motion

Unless he belly-flops

PAOLO COCCO/AFP/GETTY

10
changes

KEEP
SCORE

❏
❏
❏
❏
❏
❏
❏
❏
❏
❏

⏳
2min 45sec

Answers
on page 253

Don't Get Snookered

One of these gentlemen isn't quite on cue

0min 45sec

Answer
on page 253

CHINA PHOTOS/GETTY (2)

It's Alive!

Find the altered image and you are a dino-mite puzzler

0min 55sec

Answer
on page 254

MASTER

Sittin' on Top of the World

Some people will go to great lengths
for a little privacy

A
–
B
–
C
–
D
–
E

1   2   3   4   5

10 changes

⧗
3min 15sec

Answers
on page 254

KEEP SCORE ★ ❏ ❏ ❏ ❏ ❏ ❏ ❏ ❏ ❏ ❏

Triangulation

After you solve this puzzle,
you *will* believe in the power of pyramids

A

B

C

D

E

1   2   3   4   5

9
changes

⧗

3min 35sec

Answers
on page 254

KEEP SCORE ★ ❏ ❏ ❏ ❏ ❏ ❏ ❏ ❏ ❏

On Safari

This long-necked lady asks the universal question "Are we there yet?"

10
changes

KEEP
SCORE

⧖

3min 35sec

Answers
on page 254

One Hump or Two?

Strange days in Merrie Olde England

OLI SCARFF/GETTY

A
–
B
–
C
–
D
–
E

1 | 2 | 3 | 4 | 5

9
changes

⧗
3min 35sec

Answers
on page 254

KEEP SCORE ★ ❑ ❑ ❑ ❑ ❑ ❑ ❑ ❑ ❑

Batter Up!

Wonder if he'll slide home

PETER MCBRIDE/AURORA/GETTY

5

4

3

2

1

A — B — C — D — E

10
changes

KEEP
SCORE

❏ ❏ ❏ ❏ ❏ ❏ ❏ ❏ ❏ ❏

⏳
3min 55sec

Answers
on page 254

PICTURE PUZZLE **LIFE** | **199**

If a Tree Falls . . .
. . . Solutions must be found

A
—
B
—
C
—
D
—
E

1 | 2 | 3 | 4 | 5

9
changes

⧖
2min 50sec

Answers
on page 254

KEEP SCORE ★ ❑ ❑ ❑ ❑ ❑ ❑ ❑ ❑ ❑

The Flowers that Bloom in the Spring

This garden needs order restored

⏳
1min 35sec

Answer
on page 254

ANDREW HOLT/GETTY

KEEP SCORE

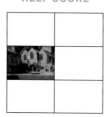

Sky High

In order to solve this, you'll need an aerial perspective

MARC TRIGALOU/GETTY

KEEP SCORE

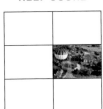

1min 15sec

Answer
on page 254

Pucker Up

Give 'em a good squeeze and you've got yourself a lot of juice

1

2

3

4

5

6

⏳
0min 35sec

Answer
on page 254

EMPORTES JM/GETTY

Big Birds

Which picture is not of a feather?

1

2

3

4

5

ZHAO JINGDONG/CHINAFOTO/GETTY

6

0min 50sec

Answer
on page 254

In the Village

This sleepy coastal hamlet is hiding a lot of secrets

DARRYL LENIUK/GETTY

12
changes

KEEP
SCORE

2min 45sec

Answers
on page 254

A — B — C — D — E

1   2   3   4   5

EXPERT

[Only serious puzzlers
dare to tread past this point.
Who's in?]

Candyland

The taffy has been pulled all out of shape

JOE BOMBA/BOMBA PHOTOS

KEEP SCORE

4min 45sec

Answer
on page 255

Fair Weather Ferry

Is this puzzle a safe harbor for you?

THOMAS MCCONVILLE/PHOTOGRAPHER'S CHOICE/GETTY

12
changes

KEEP
SCORE

4min 40sec

Answers
on page 255

Like a Neon Cowboy

If you flip the light switch, tourists will come

A

B

C

D

E

1 | 2 | 3 | 4 | 5

13
changes

KEEP
SCORE

4min 15sec

Answers
on page 255

A San Francisco Treat

Riding the cable cars is one of this city's famous offerings . . .
as is a certain rice product

A
—
B
—
C
—
D
—
E

1 | 2 | 3 | 4 | 5

13
changes

⧖

5min 25sec

Answers
on page 255

KEEP SCORE ★ ❏ ❏ ❏ ❏ ❏ ❏ ❏ ❏ ❏ ❏ ❏ ❏ ❏

Pass the Mustard

At low tide, room for a picnic

MERLE SEVERY/NATIONAL GEOGRAPHIC/GETTY

14
changes

KEEP
SCORE

5min 45sec

Answers
on page 255

Pomp and Circumstance

One of these pictures rolls a different way

1

2

3

4

5

6

1min 35sec

Answer
on page 255

CATE GILLON/GETTY

In the House of the Mouse

It's tea time at Mickey's place

1

2

3

4

5

6

BILL O'LEARY/WASHINGTON POST/GETTY

1min 45sec

Answer
on page 255

Clown Town

Even in New York City,
these folks tend to stand out

TIMOTHY A. CLARY/AFP/GETTY

A
B
C
D
E

1 | 2 | 3 | 4 | 5

14 changes

⧗

5min 35sec

Answers on page 255

KEEP SCORE ★ ❏ ❏ ❏ ❏ ❏ ❏ ❏ ❏ ❏ ❏ ❏ ❏ ❏ ❏

Mirror, Mirror on the Wall

Take a little time to reflect on this one

LOUISA GOULIAMAKI/AFP/GETTY

5 | 4 | 3 | 2 | 1

13
changes

KEEP
SCORE

⏳
5min 25sec

Answers
on page 255

A | B | C | D | E

GENIUS

[Finding a single difference
in these puzzles is a
challenge. Finding them all
might be impossible.]

Hangin' Out

The paintings aren't all that's on display

GRAEME ROBERTSON/GETTY

14 changes

KEEP SCORE

⌛

4min 30sec

Answers
on page 256

A

B

C

D

E

1   2   3   4   5

Changing of the Guard (Again)

We're not at Buckingham Palace anymore, are we?

JOHN BANAGAN/GETTY

16
changes

KEEP
SCORE

5min 25sec

Answers
on page 256

Let Me Out!

The Shuttle begs not to be mothballed

A

B

15
changes

C

☐
☐
☐
☐
☐
☐
☐
☐
☐
☐
☐
☐
☐
☐
☐

D

⏳

4min 55sec

JAMES S. M. DONNELL SPACE HANGAR

Answers
on page 256

E

1   2   3   4   5

The Curiosity Shoppe

An Anglophile would have a Dickens of a time choosing what to buy

A

B

C

D

E

1   2   3   4   5

16
changes

⧖

5min 15sec

Answers
on page 256

Merchants of Venice?

Well, there must be barbers at least, with all these poles

DAN KITWOOD/GETTY

17
changes

KEEP
SCORE

6min 25sec

Answers
on page 256

A   B   C   D   E

1   2   3   4   5

Double-Decker Fun

In Times Square, one photo doesn't quite square

1

2

3

4

5

6

0min 30sec

Answer
on page 256

PATTI MCCONVILLE/PHOTOGRAPHER'S CHOICE/GETTY

What a Small World!

Oops! Sorry!! That song playing in your head now?

1

2

3

4

5

6

JAMES P. BLAIR/NATIONAL GEOGRAPHIC/GETTY

0min 45sec

Answer
on page 256

Stick Shift

Off we go, into the wild, blue yonder . . . or not

A

B

C

D

E

1   2   3   4   5

14
changes

KEEP
SCORE

□
□
□
□
□
□
□
□
□
□
□
□
□
□

⧖
4min 15sec

Answers
on page 256

Show Time

Bright lights, Big Macs

GEORGE ROSE/GETTY

22
changes

KEEP
SCORE

7min 15sec

Answers
on page 257

LIFE

CLASSICS

[
These puzzles were
specially created with
memorable photos
from the LIFE archives.
]

Port of Call: Margaritaville

Sure looks like it

ELIOT ELISOFON/LIFE

A

—

B

—

C

—

D

—

E

1 | 2 | 3 | 4 | 5

8
changes

KEEP
SCORE

❏
❏
❏
❏
❏
❏
❏
❏

⧖
3min 15sec

Answers
on page 257

CLASSICS

Lucky Fella

He's taking his shot on the wheel of fortune

A
–
B
–
C
–
D
–
E

1   2   3   4   5

10
changes

4min 10sec

Answers
on page 257

Survivorwomen

Guests for lunch?

A

B

C

D

E

1 | 2 | 3 | 4 | 5

9
changes

KEEP
SCORE

❏
❏
❏
❏
❏
❏
❏
❏
❏

⧗
2min 15sec

Answers
on page 257

T Minus 4 and Holding

It's time to get this rocket smokin'!

NO SMOKING

J. R. EYERMAN/LIFE

ON SMOKING

A

B

C

D

E

1   2   3   4   5

8
changes

⧖
3min 40sec

Answers
on page 257

KEEP SCORE ★ ❑ ❑ ❑ ❑ ❑ ❑ ❑ ❑

You're Sure He's Friendly?

Just make sure you count your fingers after finishing this one

NINA LEEN/LIFE

A
–
B
–
C
–
D
–
E

1 | 2 | 3 | 4 | 5

12
changes

⧗

4min 50sec

Answers
on page 257

KEEP SCORE ★ ☐ ☐ ☐ ☐ ☐ ☐ ☐ ☐ ☐ ☐ ☐ ☐

ANSWERS

Finished already? Let's see how you did.

[INTRODUCTION]

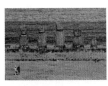

Page 135: Staring Contest
No. 1 (B1 to B2): This statue is getting a swollen head from all the attention. No. 2 (B2): It looks like someone's been doing repair work on the side. No. 3 (B3): He's flipping his (partial) head. No. 4 (B4): How does the song go, "He's got lemur eyes." No. 5 (C1): The wall is being extended. No. 6 (C3): He's so light, he floats. No. 7 (C5): Will the person who walked off with the Easter Island statue please put it back? No. 8 (D3): The itty-bitty stone has rolled away. No. 9 (E5): These tourists have gained a brand-new perspective.

[NOVICE]

Page 137: Remember to Floss No. 1 (A5 to B5): His big snout helps him sniff out tasty treats . . . like you. No. 2 (B4 to C4): Does anyone know if alligator teeth keep growing and growing? No. 3 (C1): Oh no, he used the pole as a toothpick again. No. 4 (C4): Good idea, face the giant carnivore! No. 5 (D1): His little toe is no more. No. 6 (D2): Purple makes a bold fashion statement. No. 7 (D4 to E5): Brushing helps keep the dentist away. No. 8 (E2 to E3): His dentist hopes he uses fluoridated toothpaste.

Page 138: Leap of Faith No. 1 (A3 to A5): The mountain slope has slipped away. Nos. 2 and 3 (C3): The bad plaid has caused a T-shirt temper tantrum. Watch it go purple from the bottom up. No. 4 (D2): The strap has flapped. No. 5 (D4 to D5): Would he still be grinning if he knew the cord had been cut? No. 6 (E2): Better not trust the rails around here. No. 7 (E3): He's footloose and fancy free. Or is it foot*less*?

Page 140: Land of the Giants No. 1 (B1): Ah, more back support now. Nos. 2, 3, and 4 (B3): The blue tulip is missing its friend the green shoot, while the metal strap left the barrel to join the band. Nos. 5 and 6 (C3): One side of the tablecloth is stretching down while the other side has vanished. No. 7 (C4): The fence post is toast. No. 8 (C4 to D5): This little equine looks suspiciously familiar. No. 9 (D1): When did the horse move behind the chair?

Page 142: You've Heard of the Trojan Horse? No. 1 (A1): We could say, "the bolt has bolted," but we never, ever pun. No. 2 (A3 to A4): It seems it's just the force of its personality that keeps this elephant in the air. No. 3 (B2): The shirt logo is kaput. No. 4 (C2): The plywood has been cornered. No. 5 (C4): He's put his foot down. No. 6 (D2): Now the frame runs straight and true. Nos. 7 and 8 (D3): They've painted the panel red and added a side light. No. 9 (E1): The hydraulic foot must not

be needed anymore. We very much hope it's not needed.

Page 144: Stairway to Heaven No. 1 (A3): The tower is being bricked up. No. 2 (A5 to B5): Guess what, no antenna, no radio. Nos. 3 and 4 (B2): An extra blue balloon can't keep us from thinking one of these faces looks familiar. No. 5 (B3 to B4): It looks like the builders goofed on this section of the wall. Nos. 6 and 7 (E1): Don't trip on the missing step—or the longer gown.

Page 146: Tee Time
One of the golfers in photo No. 2 must be a vampire.

Page 147: Pass the Hot Sauce
The robot in photo No. 5 broke a tooth. That's what comes from chewing on metal.

Page 148: Crazy, Dude! No. 1 (A5): Shark's fin in the water, surfers take warning. No. 2 (B2 to B3): This doggie seems goggle-eyed over the local wildlife. Nos. 3 and 4 (C3): As one pooch licks his chops, another is losing his spots. No. 5 (C4): Ear missing in action. Nos. 6 and 7 (D3): Someone's putting his best foot forward as the board loses a star. No. 8 (D4): He looks like he's got a nose for trouble.

Page 150: Pumping Canine No. 1 (A5): Smoking may be permitted here. Or not. No. 2 (B2): This place takes changing light bulbs to new heights. No. 3 (C2): She's lost her credentials. No. 4 (D1 to E1): She must be wearing mood tights. No. 5 (D2 to E2): Her pants leg is just a little long. No. 6 (E5): Trust us, no one will notice the missing stripe.

Page 152: Circle of Friends No. 1 (A4): Their safety cable is gone. Nos. 2 and 3 (B4): She's got her arm out while he's put on his ridiculous hat. He always jumps with it. No. 4 (B5): Somehow he slipped his shoe on during freefall. No. 5 (C3): Bet you didn't know that altimeters can make funny faces? No. 6 (D3): He's sticking his tongue out at the altimeter. No. 7 (D4 to E4): The backpack inclines toward purple. No. 8 (D5): The clip has gone green.

Page 154: Head Over Heels No. 1 (A1): Exit foot, stage right, or house left, that is . . . never mind. No. 2 (A5 to B5): He's got both his arms out now. No. 3 (C2): She's misplaced her belly button. No. 4 (C3): Her shirt has fallen upwards. No. 5 (D4): A logo has washed off the shirt. No. 6 (E1): Her foot has rotated all the way around. No. 7 (E2): Her sleeve is feeling a bit bluish.

Page 155: Bumper-to-Bumper Traffic No. 1 (A2): A new car is making its way *up* the twisty road. Crash, boom, bang! Can't the driver read the traffic signs? No. 2 (A2 to B3): The new elastic SUVs can stretch on demand. No. 3 (C3): Now they can lock the doors of their vehicle. No. 4 (C4): The yellow side light has been replaced with an orange one. No. 5 (D3 to D4): The hedge has been trimmed from the bottom up. No. 6 (D5): It's hard to get a handle on what's missing from this car.

Page 156: Symmetry in Stone No. 1 (B3): Over time the minaret has just faded away. Nos. 2 and 3 (B4): After the tree reached for the sky, the arch reversed itself. No. 4 (B5): The balcony has been taken down for maintenance. No. 5 (C2): These three men look like brothers. No. 6 (C3): Reflections come and go in the reflecting pool. No. 7 (D5): A twin is catching up to her sister. No. 8 (E2 to E3): It wouldn't be a LIFE Picture Puzzle book without our rubber duckie!

Page 158: Please Don't Feed the Dino No. 1 (B4): Her cap is a blank slate, or at least blank fabric. No. 2 (B5): In a common but useful picture puzzle trick, the lad has popped a button. Nos. 3 and 4 (C2): The dino has added a spot to his head while his eyes are now a shade of green. Let's hope those aren't signs of hunger. No. 5 (C3): She's added two buttons to her top. That's the last button change you will see in this book. (Liar, liar, pants on fire.) No. 6 (D1 to D2): His teeth are growing. Now we know he's hungry. No. 7 (D3 to D4): She's got diamonds on the front of her skirt. (Sing along if you know the words.) No. 8 (E3 to E4): The hem has been let down. No. 9 (E5): His shorts are suffering from droopy pant leg syndrome.

Page 160: Space Age Dubai No. 1 (A2 to B3): It's a known fact: Skyscrapers melt in the desert sun. No. 2 (C2): Count them, the parasol has three ferrules on top. No. 3 (C4 to C5): The building has lost a band. No. 4 (D2): How does the canopy stay up without its pole? Heat waves. Nos. 5 and 6 (D3): She's shed her earring and her blouse is leafing out. No. 7 (D4): Blue seems to be the color of choice for parasols. Nos. 8 and 9 (E1): An arch next door has disappeared as the parapet wall has merged together. No. 10 (E5): A shadow has fled the noonday sun.

Page 162: Flag Day No. 1 (A1 to C5): It's a rare blue-sky day on the moon. No. 2 (A5): A full moon shines down on the astronauts. Hey, wait a minute! No. 3 (B4 to C4): The lighter lunar gravity has lengthened the flag. (Okay, that makes no sense but we were hoping you wouldn't notice.) No. 4 (C1): If that's the lunar lander, then what's casting the shadow below? No. 5 (C2): We think the blue stripe looks just as nice as the red ones. No. 6 (D3): Although the flag's shadow should be longer now, somehow it's shorter. No. 7 (E2): Put that rock back where you found it. No. 8 (E3 to E4): If an astronaut's shadow reverses itself on the moon, will anyone hear it?

Page 164: What's Buggin' You? No. 1 (A4 to A5): Not only is it a giant flower, it's a giant blue flower. No. 2 (B4): The tree has grown an extra strange fruit. Nos. 3, 4, and 5 (C1): It can be hard to read a moving sign, but the exit sign is not as backwards as it used to be. On the other hand, don't these windows seem taller in the daylight? No. 6 (D3): A stealth antenna doesn't cast a shadow. No. 7 (D5): Another diner has been seated. No. 8 (E1 to E2): The bug steps forward bravely in the garden. Screams of restaurant patrons can be heard in the background.

Page 166: Fishy Business

4	1
2	3

Page 167: Everything's Coming Up Roses

4	2
1	3

Page 168: Balancing Act No. 1 (A2): The green pole has popped up. No. 2 (A3 to C3): A good unicyclist can balance facing left or right. No. 3 (A3): But how did he manage that trick with his hand? No. 4 (B5): They're cutting back the trees in the park. No. 5 (C1): A hole underneath the slide has been filled in. No. 6 (C2 to E2): Even though the pole is yellow now, that doesn't mean it's chicken. It's a pole. No. 7 (D1): Some thieves stole play equipment last night. No. 8 (D3 to E3): With cyclists riding on top, they decided to provide the bridge with extra support. No. 9 (E3): But they've moved the green pole further back. No. 10 (E5): The slide loves listening to the song "I Melt With You."

Page 170: Nice Kitties, Nice Kitties
No. 1 (A3): Everything grows rapidly in tropical climates. No. 2 (B1 to B2): Don't shoot until you see the blue of his eye. No. 3 (B4): Two whiskers have become one. No. 4 (B5): The ox has traded in its blanket for a blue one. No. 5 (C2): Did the tiger really need a longer, sharper tooth? Nos. 6 and 7 (C4): This tiger has lost a tooth. Perhaps that's why the two boys are cautiously paying a visit. No. 8 (C5): The grazing doe is winking about something. No. 9 (E4): Keep quiet about the extra toe. The tiger's quite sensitive about it.

[MASTER]

Page 173: And the Winner Is . . . No. 1 (A1): You decide: Extra cameras—neighborhood watch or Big Brother? No. 2 (A2): Two bricks had an urge to merge. No. 3 (A3): Her hat grows greener in the sunlight. No. 4 (A5): Don't flip out over the walkway sign. No. 5 (B2 to C2): It seems like a nose band bit the dust. No. 6 (C1 to C2): The wall decor is being simplified. Nos. 7 and 8 (C5): Careless, careless. Someone misspelled the town of Zirc and used the wrong color on its coat of arms. No. 9 (D2): This little horsey has a big hoof. No. 10 (D4): And this little horsey's leg is a tad short.

Page 174: Cliffhanger No. 1 (A3): And today's climb will be just a little more challenging courtesy of the famous flexible cliff. No. 2 (A3 to C3): Let's hope his backup rope is well secured. No. 3 (B5): Even climbing bags get the blues in the mountain cold. No. 4 (C5): The satchel's handle has acquired a new logo. No. 5 (D1): A cliff looms taller in the distance. No. 6 (D3): Do bigger feet help in climbing? No. 7 (D5): Logos: Easy come, easy go. Nos. 8 and 9 (E2): As the strap handles proliferate, the glacier slides over a drumlin. No. 10 (E4 to E5): The rope's shadow has been severed.

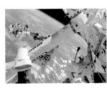

Page 176: A Walk on the Wild Side No. 1 (A3): Two shuttles in orbit at once? Nah, couldn't be. No. 2 (A3 to A4): A flange has taken up orbit all on its own. Nos. 3 and 4 (B1): In space no one can hear a 3 become an 8. Or new vent holes pop open. No. 5 (B2): Red, blue, they're all just stripes. No. 6 (C5): Two handle bars have been retrofitted as one. No. 7 (D3): Yes, yes, it's another big boot. There's an epidemic of them this year. No. 8 (D5): This must be the ninth astronaut. No. 9 (E5): And he's an astronaut without a country, or at least a flag.

Page 178: Hey There, Little Fella No. 1 (A3): My, this tree is limber. Nos. 2 and 3 (B4): Did his big ear help him hear the tree trunk disappear? No. 4 (B5): Her hair is more there. No. 5 (C2 to D2): His handler is playing peekaboo. No. 6 (C3): A bridle flashes blue. No. 7 (C4): The little guy's been given free rein. No. 8 (C5): The pink strip is being swept away. No. 9 (D1): The hoof is getting hoofier. No. 10 (D5): Now that's a horse's tail.

Page 180: Celestial Season Nos. 1 and 2 (A2): As the sarsen stone on the left gets a little taller, the nearby capstone grows a touch longer. No. 3 (A3): These capstones have joined forces. No. 4 (B4): Wait a minute! Has the heel stone vanished? Nos. 5 and 6 (B5): The cloth band has been redyed and, apparently, this isn't Stonehenge any more. Nos. 7, 8, and 9 (C3): The flower pot has moved to the left, lost its legs, and witnessed a yellow flower go pink. No. 10 (D2): She knows that a picture lasts longer. No. 11 (E4 to E5): He'd better check the ground for his missing viewfinder.

Page 182: Imperial Waters No. 1 (A4): The cupola has gently sagged down. Darn that modern prefab construction. No. 2 (B3): A green diamond has invaded the yellow ones. No. 3 (B5): The crowning ball is now quite small. No. 4 (C3 to D3): These windows have bridged the gap between. No. 5 (C5 to D5): Workers are busy extending the second floor. No. 6 (D1): He's wearing chameleon trunks. No. 7 (D2 to D3): While they were at it, the construction crew also lowered this ledge. No. 8 (D3): He's diving for pennies. Times are tough. No. 9 (D4): Very funny. Now put the sign back. No. 10 (E1): Doesn't he realize that three's a crowd. No. 11 (E4): He's slowly drifting across the pool. No. 12 (E5): The stairs are a bit grander now.

Page 184: A Slippery Slope No. 1 (A1): The new window really lets the light in. No. 2 (A3): Who keeps bricking up the walls. No. 3 (B1): Wink, wink. No. 4 (B3): Now there's more room for poster proclamations. No. 5 (C1): The barrier's been lifted. No. 6 (C3): She's got a new pretty pink hat. No. 7 (C4): His hat is getting a bit mossy. No. 8 (D1 to E1): This boy must be sliding backwards. No. 9 (D3 to D4): The icy patch is twice as slippery (and twice as big) now.

Page 186: Poetry in Motion No. 1 (A2 to B3): Lowering his arm gives him more lift on the way down. We think. No. 2 (A3): Heads up. Or head up. Whatever. No. 3 (A5 to B5): These windows make us shutter. Okay, we do use puns. Really bad ones. No. 4 (C2): The extra canopy has a secret antigravity device keeping it up. No. 5 (C3 to D4): They must be rowing backwards. No. 6 (C5): The deck looks better in brown. No. 7 (E1 to E2): Standing in boats is a good way to swamp them. No. 8 (E3): The kayak has had a quick paint job. No. 9 (E4): Santa's left the river. No. 10 (E4 to E5): But, hey, we've gained a new kayak.

Page 188: Don't Get Snookered His hand is empty in photo No. 3.

Page 189: It's Alive!
Photo No. 5 points the way to a free lunch.

Page 190: Sittin' on Top of the World
No. 1 (A2): The top triangle has blown away. No. 2 (B2): Buddha is in his shrine and all is well with the world. No. 3 (B3): Shades make the man. No. 4 (B3 to B4): Did you know that knit caps expand in low air pressure? Either that, or his skull is swelling up. No. 5 (C3 to C4): The mountain logo has been upended. No. 6 (C5 to D5): It's true. The Himalayas are still growing. No. 7 (D2): The cord and the shrine are parting ways. No. 8 (D4): Please don't use this carabiner. No. 9 (E2): The sign is not as wordy as it used to be. No. 10 (E3): Big knee pads make kneeling easier.

Page 192: Triangulation No. 1 (A3 to B4): It's a very pointy pyramid, isn't it? No. 2 (D1): The hot sun has bleached his T-shirt totally white. No. 3 (D2): Today is not a big hair day. No. 4 (D4 to D5): Try saying "blue" when it's yellow. Come on, try it. No. 5 (D5): The wheel well is no more. Nos. 6 and 7 (E3): She must be double-jointed and he's misplaced his shadow. No. 8 (E3 to E4): And her shadow has a new slant on things. No. 9 (E4): While the girl in question is suddenly feeling modest.

Page 194: On Safari No. 1 (A3): It's a rail with lofty ambitions. No. 2 (A5): Her splotches have blotched. No. 3 (C1 to D2): Safety vests don't have to be orange, do they? No. 4 (C2 to C3): His sleeve has rolled down. No. 5 (C4): Two boards got bored with being single. No. 6 (D3): For want of a bolt, a trailer was lost. Better replace it. No. 7 (D5): Two lights are better than one. No. 8 (E1): A strap has been bisected. No. 9 (E3): No light is definitely worse than one. No. 10 (E5): The word *turning* keeps turning. Well, really it's a mirror image but we like repeating *turning*.

Page 196: One Hump or Two? No. 1 (B1): The camel nods yes. No. 2 (B3): Tower Bridge is fading in the fog. No. 3 (B4): His shirt has lost its global status. No. 4 (C3): The lamp is so light, it floats in the air. No. 5 (C4): Somewhere, there's a yellow pom-pom nestled on the grass. No. 6 (C4 to D4): The man in the suit has joined the CPP, or the Camel Protection Program. But he's not a camel. We're confused. Nos. 7 and 8 (D2): As the leg gets shorter, the blanket gets longer. No. 9 (D4): This leg just gets longer.

Page 198: Batter Up! No. 1 (A1): One prayer flag seems to be swelling up. No. 2 (A3): Another flag has fluttered away. Nos. 3 and 4 (C2): Not only is the batter edging closer to the pitcher, he's also getting bigger. No. 5 (C3): Who's that in the outfield? No. 6 (C4): It seems that altitude sickness causes pitch-ers to throw the ball in the wrong direction. Nos. 7 and 8 (C5): Now why did the tent turn orange and where did that second batter come from? No. 9 (D2 to E2): Zipperless tents are the latest rage. No. 10 (D3): No one will notice one more rock on the playing field.

Page 200: If a Tree Falls . . . No. 1 (C2): The missing sign was probably used for firewood. Nos. 2 and 3 (C3): As a teenage girl clambered onto the downed tree, the tunnel began to shrink. No. 4 (D1): Her jacket has gone from hot to cool. No. 5 (D2): A rock is taking a rest at the edge of the road. No. 6 (D3): Doesn't that boy know there's a camper heading toward him? No. 7 (D5): The front of the station wagon has been chopped off. Nos. 8 and 9 (E4): The license plate thief has been busy while Mr. Bad Directions has been playing with this sign.

Page 202: The Flowers that Bloom in the Spring

6	3
5	4
2	1

Page 203: Sky High

4	5
2	3
6	1

Page 204: Pucker Up
In photo No. 6 a palm tree doesn't grow at this festival.

Page 205: Big Birds
His pants are minus a stripe in photo No. 2.

Page 206: In the Village No. 1 (A2): The headlands are heading out to sea. No. 2 (A3): The lighthouse has been built up. No. 3 (A4 to B4): To handle all the crowds, the government is lengthening the building. No. 4 (B3 to B4): The lobster boat looks to be ahead of schedule. No. 5 (C2 to D2): The pole has vaulted away. No. 6 (C3 to D3): Look away for a moment and a chimney disappears. No. 7 (D2): As part of the green movement, the church is relying more on natural light. No. 8 (D3): The barn door is also going green. No. 9 (E2): The house has gained a win-

dow. No. 10 (E3): And lost a chair. No. 11 (E4): Please don't fence off the street. No. 12 (E5): Window installation has hit this town in a big way.

[EXPERT]

Page 209: Candyland

3	8	1
9	5	7
6	2	4

Page 210: Fair Weather Ferry No. 1 (A2): A skyscraper has flipped its top. Nos. 2 and 3 (B1): The building has racked up more floors but lost its corporate sponsorship. No. 4 (B3): Instead of a lady, the building vanishes—at least partly. No. 5 (B5 to C5): This place has more window offices now. No. 6 (C1): Really wide windows usually mean executive suites. No. 7 (C2): This little dormer climbs up the roof. No. 8 (C3 to D3): While this little dormer falls off. No. 9 (D3): The red speedboat seems a little seasick. No. 10 (D4): The palm has been replanted behind the RV. No. 11 (E2): A boat motored away. No. 12 (E5): And a buoy bobs.

Page 212: Like a Neon Cowboy No. 1 (A2 to A3): Anybody got a match? No. 2 (A3): With a thumb like this, he must be good at hitchhiking. No. 3 (B1 to C1): More lights mean brighter nights. No. 4 (B4): With this camera, LVPD really sees all. No. 5 (C3): His spur's done gone. No. 6 (C5): This boot was made for kicking. No. 7 (D2): The hyphen pivots. Nos. 8 and 9 (D3): The store has sold all but one of its gifts and someone flipped an *S*. No. 10 (D4): Who tore the poster down? No. 11 (E2): He's 78 now. He looks good for his age. No. 12 (E4): Don't try to sit on this stool. What stool? Exactly. No. 13 (E5): Are you experienced?

Page 214: A San Francisco Treat No. 1 (A4): The two tall stacks are on top of it all, or at least on top of the street. No. 2 (B3): Let's hope the missing vent isn't really necessary. No. 3 (C3): The new windows are low-riders. No. 4 (C4): Someone shut the window. Nos. 5 and 6 (D1): One vehicle sports three headlights and the orange car is moving up fast. No. 7 (D2): Once again, it's so easy to spin a "6" into a "9." No. 8 (D4 to E4): The Powell and Market sign tries to center itself. No. 9 (D4): Number 4 is no more. No. 10 (D5): The hydrant has a twin. No. 11 (E1): The road repair crew has repaired the repair. No. 12 (E2): The cable car's plow is whole, we mean it has no hole. No. 13 (E3): A manhole cover has been covered.

Page 216: Pass the Mustard Nos. 1 and 2 (A2): The antenna goes down as the piling goes up. No. 3 (B1): Don't frown but there's an extra skiff in town. No. 4 (B4 to B5): A cabin cruiser cruises home. No. 5 (C4): He's eating a mega-dog. Nos. 6 and 7 (D2): Can you handle it? The bag's handle will no longer

serve, while the pot's handle hides behind Mom's leg. No. 8 (D3): Does she realize that she's got a dog in the pot and on the bun? No. 9 (D5): Even if he notices that it's missing, chances are that he'll never find his watch in all that sand. No. 10 (E1): A cantaloupe has joined the picnic. No. 11 (E2 to E3): The reflection is a reflection of itself. No. 12 (E3): Redundancy in planning: There are four people and five cups. No. 13 (E4): His pant leg dangles down. No. 14 (E5): He's digging his foot out of the sand.

Page 218: Pomp and Circumstance One of the wheels in photo No. 5 must be in the shop for repair.

Page 219: In the House of the Mouse Mickey must be rolling his eyes in photo No. 4.

Page 220: Clown Town No. 1 (A2): Neuhaus is new now. Or at least, its signage is new. Get it? No. 2 (A5): Turn right, no, turn left. No. 3 (B2): If green thumbs signify good gardeners, what do green noses indicate? Don't answer that. Nos. 4 and 5 (B3): A new stranger in the crowd seems to disapprove of the clown with vulcan ears. No. 6 (B4): A jacket stud has flip-flopped. Nos. 7 and 8 (C3): The clowns broke their chains and grabbed a poster to celebrate their freedom. No. 9 (C4): His glockenspiel jacket now goes one note lower. Plink, plink, plonk. No. 10 (C5 to D5): Her, um, er, his stockings are a lovely shade of green now. No. 11 (C5): Ouch! A sneaker's been surgically removed. No. 12 (D5): My, what a big foot you have! Is it better to stomp with? No. 13 (E2): These cuffs are very yellow—and very tall. No. 14 (E3 to E4): The post has been repositioned and significantly elongated. *E-l-o-n-g-a-t-e-d*, now isn't that just an elongated way of saying lengthened? Hmmmm, nine letters, ten letters, never mind.

Page 222: Mirror, Mirror on the Wall No. 1 (A1): Now there's a reflector behind the reflections. No. 2 (A2): The light in the mirror is no more. No. 3 (B1 to C1): The stripes on his shirt are a lovely shade of mustard now. By the way, we're lying about the lovely. No. 4 (B2): Either the beret is getting bigger or his head has been shrunk. No. 5 (B3 to C4): The reflection in this mirror is a mirror-mirror image. It's like a double-negative in English. Or not. No. 6 (B4 to C4): The man in the mirror is getting closer and closer. Nos. 7 and 8 (B4): One of these mirrors has borrowed the reflection of the man previously mentioned to replace the reflection of the frame of the other mirror. Do you find all these mirrors as confusing as we do? No. 9 (B5): The jet has flown past the frame. But where are all those little people going to stay? No. 10 (C2): Longer horns produce louder notes. No. 11 (C4): Someone's ducked out of the reflection. No. 12 (D2): His footstep casts no shadow. No. 13 (E3 to E4): The heat of the Grecian sun is softening the brass.

[GENIUS]

Page 225: Hangin' Out No. 1 (A1 to B1): Without flowers, you don't need a vase. No. 2 (A2 to B2): Elastic paintings can be *s-t-r-e-t-c-h-e-d* to fit. No. 3 (A3): His new wool cap fits perfectly. No. 4 (A5): Who's to say which way is up. No. 5 (B2): Clearly, fame has gone to his head. No. 6 (B3): He must be practicing sign language. No. 7 (C1): The cherub is cavorting. No. 8 (C2): Does *Dad Peace* mean no yelling? Probably not. No. 9 (C5): He doesn't look it, but he should be more comfortable without a tie. No. 10 (D1): She's got a fan, a big fan. No. 11 (D3): The storm tossed the ship to and fro. No. 12 (E2): Wild animal alert! The wood trim has become beaver fodder. No. 13 (E4): This painting is so weighty, it's sagged to the floor. No. 14 (E5): Long aprons appear to be "in" this year.

Page 226: Changing of the Guard (Again) Nos. 1 and 2 (A1): Part of the roof has drooped over the edge and a lotus blossom tile has fallen off. Nos. 3 and 4 (A3 to B3): Graffiti artists have been messing with the logograms. No. 5 (A4): Someone's stuck up an extra tile here. No. 6 (C1): Two bricks, two bricks, two bricks are one. No. 7 (C2): If you're going to wear a yellow hat, it might as well be tall. No. 8 (C3): The top of his helmet has visibility fatigue. No. 9 (C5): He's quite a tall gent. Nos. 10 and 11 (D2): This horn won't blow and his beard looks fake. No. 12 (D3): Here's a tip, the rod has lost its . . . tip. No. 13 (D4): On the other hand, Gabriel can really make *this* horn blow. The guy is named Gabriel. Don't ask us how we know. We know. No. 14 (D5): His costume billows in the breeze. No. 15 (E1): He's so light, he doesn't need feet. No. 16 (E4): It's a mega-ribbon.

Page 228: Let Me Out! Nos. 1, 2, and 3 (A3): There are more stars on the longer field of blue but one has slipped off, and the shuttle's tail rises high to the, well, not sky. No. 4 (A4 to B4): The satellite has tacked on an extension. No. 5 (A5): An astronaut floats freely near the . . . roof. It just doesn't have the same ring to it. No. 6 (B3): American flags don't sag, they just get longer. No. 7 (C2): Better not try a wheelie now. No. 8 (C3): They're shy one porthole. That's what it's called, right? No. 9 (C4): The display case quite a hangover, I mean overhang. No. 10 (D2): Has anyone seen a darlin' little *c*? No. 11 (D3): Without its foot, an *L* is just an *I*. Oh my. No. 12 (E1): The spot is bare of chair. No. 13 (E2): He's shambling toward the right. No. 14 (E3): Mission Control, we have liftoff. No. 15 (E4): This kid comes from the Land of Mirrors.

Page 230: The Curiosity Shoppe No. 1 (A2): He knows when to keep his mouth shut. Nos. 2 and 3 (A3): Will Mr. Nosy notice the needlessly missing horn on the opposite wall? No. 4 (A4): These wooden skis are the extra-large model with jumbo splinters. No. 5 (B1): The person who buys this uniform better know how to sew. No. 6 (B2): Swap a *P* for a *B* and you have a whole different kind of mushroom. No. 7 (B3): A customer must have bought the blue letter *A*. No. 8 (B4): The wooden soldier is suffering from some shrinkage. No. 9 (C2 to D2): These days the good old Union Jack is feeling a little blue. No. 10 (C5 to D5): Yellow is the new red, at least for

hats. No. 11 (D1): My, grandmother. What a big putter you have. Nos. 12 and 13 (D2): From the look of these two signs, English may not be this storekeeper's forte. No. 14 (D3): The floor has been stripe-swiped. No. 15 (E1): The shaft has a bigger grip now. And we don't mean anything by that. No. 16 (D5 to E5): The hat looks even more ridiculous now.

Page 232: Merchants of Venice? No. 1 (B4 to C4): The sun wheel spins. All is well with the universe. No. 2 (B5): Guess who joined the Chimney Relocation Program? Nos. 3 and 4 (C1): We're two flags up and one chimney down. Nos. 5 and 6 (C2): With one building losing a window, the cathedral decrees "Let the light in." No. 7 (C3): No matter how you spell it, Venice always starts with a *V*, doesn't it? No. 8 (C3 to D3): He's surrounded by horns. No. 9 (C4): The stacks look overstacked. No. 10 (D1): Every now and then you have to be daring and try a different-colored spiral. No. 11 (D2): The red poles are reaching for the sky. No. 12 (E1): This powerboat is going incognito—and numberless. No. 13 (E1 to E2): There's more oar than before. No. 14 (E2): The rumors about the pole's translucentness are baseless. Or is it the pole that is baseless? No. 15 (E3 to E4): Swell, the boat's hit a swell. No. 16 (E3): And it's lost its reflection. No. 17 (E4): Do they have one more lion to roar or one more mouth to feed?

Page 234: Double-Decker Fun The big blue LG sign in Photo No. 1 is one dot down. Yes, yes, it's a very small change but this is the Genius section, isn't it? (Is it? Better check.Okay, yes it is.) So deal with it.

Page 235: What a Small World! The lad has pulled in his arm in photo No. 6. Check it out, it's really there . . . or not there. You know what we mean. But do we?

Page 236: Stick Shift No. 1 (A2 to A4): The numbers are button-swapping. No. 2 (A3): The words on the trim gauge are getting into a similar game. No. 3 (B1): This knob only looks more important than the rest. Nos. 4 and 5 (B2): The arrow hand is supposed to turn, not the whole dial! How nice, a lap counter. There must be a pool in the back of the plane—where the engine's supposed to be. No. 6 (B3): For want of a screw, a cockpit was lost. No. 7 (C5): Does anyone know what this extra light is for? No. 8 (C5 to D5): Let's hope we won't need the missing lever later. Otherwise, we just got shafted. Nos. 9 and 10 (D1): A taller toggle isn't necessarily abnormal, but someone labelled it that way. No. 11 (D3): The approach label is approaching the middle. No. 12 (D4): Someone flipped the switch but not the shadow. No. 13 (E4): There's a brand-new switch to fiddle with. No. 14 (E5): The dial has lost its stripe.

Page 238: **Show Time** No. 1 (A1): These days, one window less looks out on old Broadway. Nos. 2 and 3 (A1 to B1): Don't fear the power of the green arm or you, too, will face an impossible date! No. 4 (A1): Copy's been busy rewriting the subhead. No. 5 (A2): The *N* is feeling a bit backward today. No. 6 (A2 to B3): Sure thing, the sign's been redesigned. No. 7 (A3): Click! Lights on in the office. No. 8 (A4 to B4): Click! Lights off in this one. No. 9 (A5): Someone's got a nice big office with a picture window now. No. 10 (B2 to C2): You've got to be kidding! They really can't spell PALACE? No. 11 (B2): It's a funny-looking *E*. No. 12 (B5): It's amazing that they got rid of even one light. Of course, one can't tell the difference, can one? No. 13 (C1): The mask is blind to all the glitter and glamour. No. 14 (C3): The streetlight is a twin. No. 15 (C4 to C5): The golden arches hang down in the middle. No. 16 (D2 to D3): It's a scavenger hunt. Next we find a missing THE. Nos. 17, 18, and 19 (D3): The lamp pole has used vanishing cream from *The Body Shop*, Times Square Information has lost its center, and the *i* is head over heels. No. 20 (D3 to E3): The excess vanishing cream has dripped down on the wheel. No. 21 (D5): The taxi ad must be designed to be read in a rearview mirror—but it's on the side of the car. No. 22 (E5): You didn't hear it from us, but big bumpers come in handy with New York City drivers.

[LIFE CLASSICS]

Page 241: **Port of Call: Margaritaville**
No. 1 (A1 to B2): Without wind, more sail won't help. No. 2 (B2 to C2): Who turned on the Klingon cloaking shield? Shut it down before the mast disappears altogether. No. 3 (C1): One of the mooring lines slipped off. No. 4 (C5): Another boat has dropped anchor. No. 5 (D2): The hyphen is migrating up. No. 6 (E2): A dangling rope dangles lower. No. 7 (E2 to E3): The pile has rotted away. No. 8 (E3): It looks like the shadow repair crew has been at work here.

Page 242: **Lucky Fella** No. 1 (A2): It's dangerous to jump off when the ferris wheel is in motion but it seems he did it anyway. No. 2 (A3): In a blink of an eye, a sister became a stranger. No. 3 (A4 to A5): The bolt's been sheared away. No. 4 (B1 to B2): An extra crossbar has been added. No. 5 (B3 to C3): The end of the footrest has been capped. No. 6 (B5): It's a bigger spaceship now. No. 7 (C1): Naw, that was a spare girder. No. 8 (C3 to D3): Was that the sound of a snapping cable? No. 9 (D1 to E1): Curfew rules: No one leaves this trailer until we draw the door back in. No one. Got that? No. 10 (D4): For fairs that move around every week, it helps to have everything clearly labelled and numbered.

Page 244: **Survivorwomen** No. 1 (B1): We cannot tell a lie. We photochopped down this cherry tree. Except it wasn't cherry. Nos. 2 and 3 (B3): A bear asks the silent question, "Got milk?" and a camper is blissfully unaware that her pan can't be handled. No. 4 (B5): The boulder has a bigger shoulder. No. 5 (C2): The new thermos keeps a lot more cool. No. 6 (C3): Did the bear get the milk? No. 7 (C3 to C4): Her sleeve has slipped. No. 8 (D1): The plate has been unclipped. No. 9 (D5): The can slides into view.

Page 246: **T Minus 4 and Holding** No. 1 (B2): Watch out, the rocket's been untethered. Blast-off imminent! Nos. 2 and 3 (C2): Gain a stripe and lose a lamp. It's about even-steven. No. 4 (D2): I've been through the desert on a rocket with no number. No, that's not quite right. Back to square one. No. 5 (D3 to D4): On smoking, everything goes kaboom! No. 6 (E1): It's a big, old garbage barrel, and even bigger now. No. 7 (E2): The fuel truck has shed its chains. No. 8 (E5): Don't worry, that's just a left-over leg from the last test flight.

Page 248: **You're Sure He's Friendly?** Nos. 1 and 2 (A2): He's got a big collar and really, really big hair. No. 3 (A2 to A3): The cable's down again ... but this one doesn't have anything to do with the Internet. No. 4 (A3 to B3): Bet he's really proud of his horns. No. 5 (B3 to C3): A nose like this is meant for sniffing. No. 6 (C1): He's tucked his shirt in.
No. 7 (C2): Another darn rope snapped. No. 8 (C5): On hot days, palm trees pull up their trunks inside their fronds. If you believe that, we've got a bridge in Brooklyn that's for sale. No. 9 (D1 to E1): How hot is it? It's so hot, the sun is burning away the shadows. No. 10 (D5): Hope you didn't have anything at stake at these coordinates. Get it? Har, har! No. 11 (E2): Lately, many giraffes are flocking to Hollywood plastic surgeons to get their hooves uncloven. No. 12 (D4 to E4): His leg strap has been unwrapped.

Synchronized Walking

You know what they say, "The bigger they are, the harder they fall."

CARSTEN KOALL/GETTY

14 changes

KEEP SCORE

4min 25sec

A — B — C — D — E

1   2   3   4   5

Solve this and become a true puppet, I mean, puzzle master.

ANSWERS No. 1 (A1 to B1): The tackle's been snipped. **No. 2 (A4):** A flag flaps freely in the breeze. **No. 3 (A5):** It's true, Alice. There are growth hormones for statues. **No. 4 (B2):** The tackle is still there but, say goodbye to the block. **No. 5 (B3):** The statue lifted up her skirts and sashayed away. **No. 6 (C1):** The lamp has fading lamp disease. **No. 7 (C3):** A window descends. **No. 8 (C5):** Let the arrows (or are they wings?) point the way. **No. 9 (D1):** He must be a member of the Hair Club for Men. **No. 10 (E1):** Don't shake hands with this fellow. **No. 11 (E2):** She's got no sole. **Nos. 12 and 13 (E4):** Water has nowhere to drain and the stripe has split asunder. **No. 14 (E5):** This guy's popped a button.

LIFE

THE EXTRAORDINARY

PICTURE PUZZLE

CAN YOU SPOT THE DIFFERENCES?

THE 12TH BOOK IN THE WILDLY POPULAR SERIES

4 LEVELS: NOVICE · MASTER · EXPERT · GENIUS

WELCOME TO LIFE'S TWELFTH PICTURE PUZZLE BOOK

Who would have thunk it? When we released our first LIFE Picture Puzzle book all those years ago, we suspected we were on to a good thing, and when it went to number one on *The New York Times* best-seller list, we were suitably thrilled. But we had no idea that, 12 books later, the franchise would still be going strong. To paraphrase the words of a famous Oscar winner, "You like us, you really like us." And we like you: We feel it's a privilege to continue to craft these puzzles, and it feels like we're getting back together with old friends as we issue this twelfth book in the series.

When our team started to plan the new book, all sorts of ideas for a new theme were tossed around. The word *extraordinary* kept coming up: "Isn't it extraordinary—12 books." "It's extraordinary how much people like these puzzles—kids and adults alike." Going with what was in the air, we asked our photo editors to start looking for extraordinary—and extraordinarily fun—images from around the world. They came up with many surprising, wonderful pictures, and we sat down to work. On the pages that follow is the result, and it's fair to say that we are just as proud of this book as we were of our first.

The theme may be new, but the hallmarks of the LIFE Picture Puzzle series haven't changed. Our Novice section is still a kind of tutorial, wherein we present the easiest puzzles for our beginning players. Our Master and Expert sections slowly dial up the difficulty, preparing you for the increasingly difficult challenges to come. Then there's our Genius section. We feel we should give you fair warning about this chapter: The Genius puzzles are so difficult that even our Puzzle Master sometimes has trouble finding all the changes when he returns for a second or third look. And he's the one who hid them in the first place!

[OUR CUT-UP PUZZLES: EASY AS 1-2-3]

We snipped a photo into four or six pieces. Then we rearranged the pieces and numbered them.

Your mission: Beneath each cut-up puzzle, write the number of the piece in the box where it belongs.

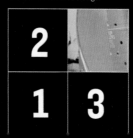

Check the answer key at the back of the book to see what the reassembled image looks like.

[HOW TO PLAY THE PUZZLES]

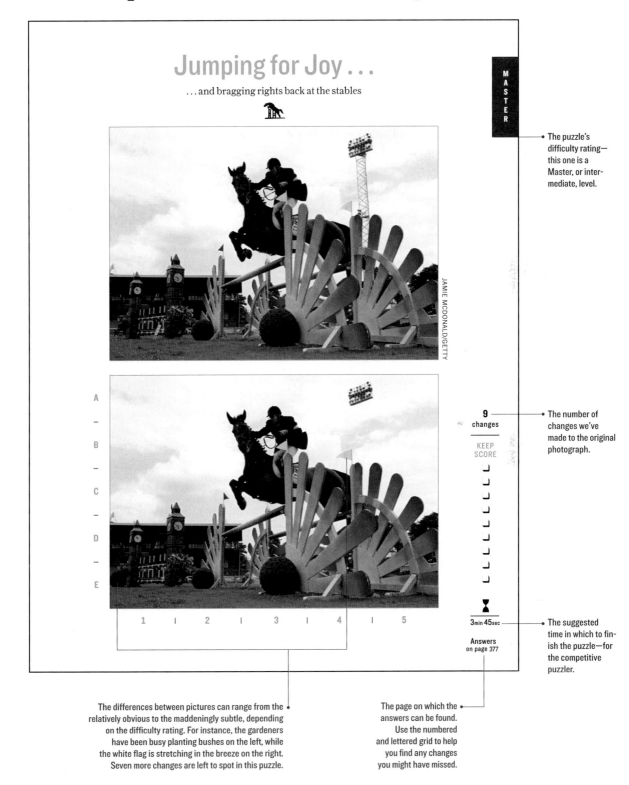

Jumping for Joy . . .

. . . and bragging rights back at the stables

MASTER

JAMIE MCDONALD/GETTY

The puzzle's difficulty rating—this one is a Master, or intermediate, level.

9 changes

The number of changes we've made to the original photograph.

KEEP SCORE

3min 45sec

Answers on page 377

The suggested time in which to finish the puzzle—for the competitive puzzler.

The differences between pictures can range from the relatively obvious to the maddeningly subtle, depending on the difficulty rating. For instance, the gardeners have been busy planting bushes on the left, while the white flag is stretching in the breeze on the right. Seven more changes are left to spot in this puzzle.

The page on which the answers can be found. Use the numbered and lettered grid to help you find any changes you might have missed.

NOVICE

[
These puzzles are for everyone:
rookies and veterans,
young and old. Start here, and
sharpen your skills.
]

Baa, Baa, Yellow Sheep

This puzzle's dyed in the wool

JON FURNISS/WIREIMAGE/GETTY

A
—
B
—
C
—
D
—
E

1 | 2 | 3 | 4 | 5

7
changes

KEEP
SCORE

❏
❏
❏
❏
❏
❏
❏

⧗

1min 50sec

Answers
on page 377

Head Shot

Sometimes getting a good photo requires
a change of perspective

BEN STANSALL/AFP/GETTY

A
—
B
—
C
—
D
—
E

1 | 2 | 3 | 4 | 5

9
changes

⧗
2min 35sec

Answers
on page 377

I, Robot

You, puny puzzle-solving humans

6
changes

KEEP
SCORE

❏
❏
❏
❏
❏
❏

⧗
1min 45sec

Answers
on page 377

One-Trick Pony

If they cross the finish line together,
does it still count?

MOHAMMED MAHJOUB/AFP/GETTY

A
—
B
—
C
—
D
—
E

1 | 2 | 3 | 4 | 5

7 changes

⧖

2min 25sec

Answers
on page 377

KEEP SCORE ★ ❏ ❏ ❏ ❏ ❏ ❏ ❏

Sky Jockey

She's spinning more than just her wheels

AFP/GETTY

A

B

C

D

E

1　　　　2　　　　3　　　　4　　　　5

9
changes

⏳
2min 40sec

Answers
on page 377

KEEP SCORE ★ ❏ ❏ ❏ ❏ ❏ ❏ ❏ ❏ ❏

As He Takes Flight

You flag the photo that doesn't fit

0min 25sec

Answer
on page 377

PIERRE-PHILIPPE MARCOU/AFP/GETTY

Group Bliss

These couples are perfect matches, and so are five of the pictures

STR/AFP/GETTY

0min 40sec

Answer
on page 377

Puttin' On the Ritz

This family is all dressed up *and* has somewhere to go

PATRICK HERTZOG/AFP/GETTY

8
changes

KEEP
SCORE

❏
❏
❏
❏
❏
❏
❏
❏

⏳
2min 20sec

Answers
on page 377

Horsing Around

Who's the beast of burden here?

TIM GRAHAM/GETTY

A

—

B

—

C

—

D

—

E

1 | 2 | 3 | 4 | 5

6
changes

⏳
2min 15sec

Answers
on page 377

KEEP SCORE ★ ❑ ❑ ❑ ❑ ❑ ❑

Must-See TV

He's not your standard couch potato

CARLO ALLEGRI/GETTY

A
—
B
—
C
—
D
—
E

1 2 3 4 5

8
changes

⧗

2min 45sec

Answers
on page 377

KEEP SCORE ★ ❑ ❑ ❑ ❑ ❑ ❑ ❑ ❑

Sunday in the Park...

... with Rex

NORBERT MILLAUER/AFP/GETTY

8
changes

2min 35sec

Answers
on page 378

A
—
B
—
C
—
D
—
E

1   2   3   4   5

In Search of Perfect Powder

Boldly going where no skier has gone before

LEO MASON/IMAGE BANK/GETTY

A
—
B
—
C
—
D
—
E

1 | 2 | 3 | 4 | 5

6
changes

KEEP
SCORE

⌣ ⌣ ⌣ ⌣ ⌣ ⌣

⧗

3min 25sec

Answers
on page 378

Catch of the Day

There's a lot that's fishy about this photo

A

B

C

D

E

1 2 3 4 5

9
changes

Answers
on page 378

Guardian Angel

Everyone feels safer with their flying pig
patrolling up above

A

B

C

D

E

1   2   3   4   5

11
changes

⧗

4min 10sec

Answers
on page 378

KEEP SCORE ★ ❏ ❏ ❏ ❏ ❏ ❏ ❏ ❏ ❏ ❏ ❏

Hitchhikers in the Sky

Either that or the flight was overbooked

DIGITAL VISION/GETTY

A

B

C

D

E

1   2   3   4   5

10
changes

⧗
3min 50sec

Answers
on page 378

KEEP SCORE ★ ❏ ❏ ❏ ❏ ❏ ❏ ❏ ❏ ❏ ❏ ❏

House of Slytherin?

Let's hope they can parse Parseltongue

HANK WALKER/LIFE

A
—
B
—
C
—
D
—
E

1 | 2 | 3 | 4 | 5

9
changes

KEEP
SCORE

❏
❏ ❏
❏ ❏
❏
❏ ❏
❏ ❏
❏
❏

⧗
3min 15sec

Answers
on page 378

Hold On Tight!

From this point on, it's all downhill

A

B

C

D

E

1   2   3   4   5

8
changes

⌛
3min 30sec

Answers
on page 378

KEEP SCORE ★ ☐ ☐ ☐ ☐ ☐ ☐ ☐ ☐

Party Girls, GOP-Style

Yes, it's true. They like Ike.

ED CLARK/LIFE

A

B

C

D

E

1   2   3   4   5

10
changes

KEEP
SCORE

❏
❏
❏
❏
❏
❏
❏
❏
❏
❏

⧗

2min 55sec

Answers
on page 378

Hoping for the Big Bounce

Can you reconnect the biker to his bungee cord before sudden impact?

⧗ 0min 25sec

Answer
on page 378

KEEP SCORE

Superhero in Training

Here's a second high-flyer who needs help

OLIVIER RENCK/AURORA/GETTY

KEEP SCORE

0min 45sec

Answer
on page 378

All Eyes on Big Ben

The times they are a-changin' in olde London towne

CARL DE SOUZA/AFP/GETTY

5 | 4 | 3 | 2 | 1

A | B | C | D | E

12
changes

KEEP
SCORE

⊔
⊔
⊔
⊔
⊔
⊔
⊔
⊔
⊔
⊔
⊔
⊔

⏳
4min 25sec

Answers
on page 378

MASTER

[
Here, puzzles get
a little harder. You'll
need to raise
your game a level.
]

In the Pink

It's smooth sailing for this funny bunny

ISIFA/LIBOR FOJTIK/GETTY

11
changes

KEEP
SCORE

A

—

B

—

C

—

D

—

E

1 | 2 | 3 | 4 | 5

4min 25sec

Answers
on page 379

Risky Business

He goes bang for a living, five times a day

A

B

C

D

E

1 | 2 | 3 | 4 | 5

9
changes

KEEP
SCORE

❏
❏
❏
❏
❏
❏
❏
❏
❏

⧗

3min 45sec

Answers
on page 379

Talk About a Hybrid

This is the perfect house for someone always on the go

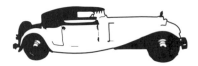

A
—
B
—
C
—
D
—
E

1 | 2 | 3 | 4 | 5

11
changes

⧗
3min 15sec

Answers
on page 379

KEEP SCORE ★ ❏ ❏ ❏ ❏ ❏ ❏ ❏ ❏ ❏ ❏ ❏

When Pigs Fly . . .

. . . so will I

STR/AFP/GETTY

A

—

B

—

C

·

—

D

—

E

1 | 2 | 3 | 4 | 5

9
changes

⏳

3min 25sec

Answers
on page 379

KEEP SCORE ★ ❏ ❏ ❏ ❏ ❏ ❏ ❏ ❏ ❏

On the Monkey Bars

Where's the missing link between the two gymnasts?

KOEN VAN WEEL/AFP/GETTY

5

4

3

2

1

9
changes

⏳

2min 55sec

Answers
on page 379

A | B | C | D | E

Ding-Dong! The Witch Is Dead

She's not only merely dead,
she's really most sincerely dead

TIMOTHY A. CLARY/AFP/GETTY

A
—
B
—
C
—
D
—
E

1 | 2 | 3 | 4 | 5

10
changes

⧗
_____
3min 40sec

Answers
on page 379

KEEP SCORE ★ ❑ ❑ ❑ ❑ ❑ ❑ ❑ ❑ ❑ ❑

Not-So-Skinny Dipping

In Japan, things are going swimmingly for these two

A
—
B
—
C
—
D
—
E

1 | 2 | 3 | 4 | 5

12
changes

KEEP
SCORE

❑
❑
❑
❑
❑
❑
❑
❑
❑
❑
❑
❑

⧖

3min 55sec

Answers
on page 379

Horns of Plenty

Reminds us of a certain cough drop commercial

THOMAS LOHNES/AFP/GETTY

10
changes

KEEP
SCORE

❑ ❑ ❑ ❑ ❑ ❑ ❑ ❑ ❑ ❑

⏳
3min 35sec

Answers
on page 379

Caution! Baby (Giraffe) Onboard

This little lady's definitely a head-turner

A
–
B
–
C
–
D
–
E

1   2   3   4   5

9
changes

⧗
2min 50sec

Answers
on page 379

KEEP SCORE ★ ❏ ❏ ❏ ❏ ❏ ❏ ❏ ❏ ❏

Making Like Jonah

This exhibit tells a whale of a tale

JAN JOHANNESSEN/GETTY

A
—
B
—
C
—
D
—
E

1 | 2 | 3 | 4 | 5

10
changes

⧗

3min 25sec

Answers
on page 380

KEEP SCORE ★ ❏ ❏ ❏ ❏ ❏ ❏ ❏ ❏ ❏ ❏

Traffic Jam

Can you spot which picture sails away from the others?

1

2

3

4

5

6

0min 35sec

Answer
on page 380

CARLOS ALVAREZ/GETTY

Doggie Diplomacy

Five pooches vote "Aye," one votes "Nay"

1

2

3

4

5

6

LUCAS DAWSON/GETTY

0min 50sec

Answer
on page 380

And the Band Played On

Here's hoping they finish before the tide comes in

10
changes

KEEP
SCORE

❏
❏
❏
❏
❏
❏
❏
❏
❏
❏

⧗

3min 25sec

Answers
on page 380

Tipping Point

Time to sue the architect!

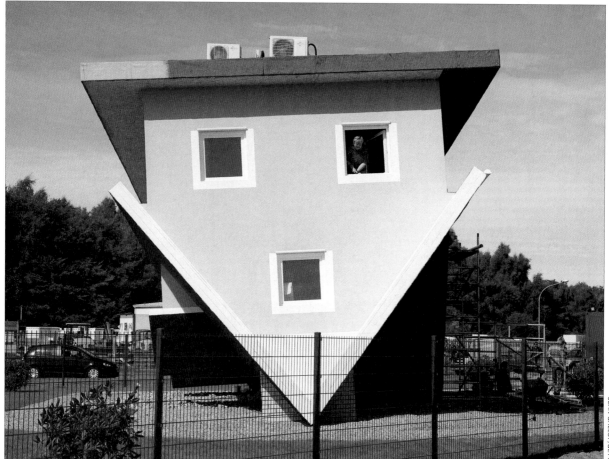

A
—
B
—
C
—
D
—
E

1 | 2 | 3 | 4 | 5

9
changes

⏳
3min 55sec

Answers
on page 380

KEEP SCORE ★ ❑ ❑ ❑ ❑ ❑ ❑ ❑ ❑ ❑ ❑

Spin Cycle

Around and around he goes

10
changes

KEEP
SCORE

❑ ❑ ❑ ❑ ❑ ❑ ❑ ❑ ❑ ❑

⧗

4min **15**sec

Answers
on page 380

Canal Concerto

Find the altered image and you can toot your own horn

1min 15sec

Answer
on page 380

MARCO SABADIN/AFP/GETTY

The Weather Outside Is Frightful

But come on in, the water's fine

1

2

3

4

5

SEAN GALLUP/GETTY

6

1min 10sec

Answer
on page 380

Flipping Flapjacks

As in most things, practice makes perfect

MATT CARDY/GETTY

A
—
B
—
C
—
D
—
E

1   2   3   4   5

9
changes

⏳
3min 35sec

Answers
on page 380

Moving Day

You're the contractor, now build the house

1min 45sec

Answer
on page 380

KEEP SCORE

Don't Look Down Now

Acrophobics may want to skip this puzzle

MASTER

SCOTT OLSON/GETTY

1min 10sec

Answer
on page 380

KEEP SCORE

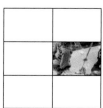

Birds Do It, Bees Do It

Even statues in the trees do it

CHUNG SUNG-JUN/GETTY

5 — 4 — 3 — 2 — 1

A | B | C | D | E

12
changes

KEEP
SCORE

☐ ☐ ☐ ☐ ☐ ☐ ☐ ☐ ☐ ☐ ☐ ☐

⧗
3min 50sec

Answers
on page 380

EXPERT

[
Only serious puzzlers
dare to tread past this point.
Who's in?
]

Some Really Great Pumpkins

Where is Linus when you need him?

EXPERT

KEEP SCORE

3min 45sec

Answer
on page 381

Stupid Human Tricks

Just feed him candy and he'll roll over every time

BEN HIDER/GETTY

A

B

C

D

E

1 | 2 | 3 | 4 | 5

13
changes

KEEP
SCORE

❏
❏
❏
❏
❏
❏
❏
❏
❏
❏
❏
❏
❏

⌛

4min 10sec

Answers
on page 381

A Hair-Raising Competition

Talk about a stiff upper lip

WILDBILD/AFP/GETTY

5 | 4 | 3 | 2 | 1

A | B | C | D | E

12
changes

KEEP
SCORE

3min 50sec

Answers
on page 381

Rack 'Em Up

Can you run the table on this puzzle?

15
changes

KEEP
SCORE

4min 35sec

Answers
on page 381

Gourds A-Plenty

Five sets are the same. Which isn't?

1

2

3

4

5

6

1min 45sec

Answer
on page 381

LIBOR FOJTIK/ISIFA/GETTY

Be-Side Saddle

He's either performing a stunt or looking for a high five

1

2

3

4

5

6

FERENC ISZA/AFP/GETTY

2min 5sec

Answer
on page 381

Spick-and-Span

As they say, cleanliness is next to clownliness

13
changes

KEEP
SCORE

4min 45sec

Answers
on page 381

REM

These kids are keeping their eye on you

SCOTT OLSON/GETTY

A
–
B
–
C
–
D
–
E

1 | 2 | 3 | 4 | 5

14
changes

4min 50sec

Answers
on page 381

KEEP SCORE ★ ❑ ❑ ❑ ❑ ❑ ❑ ❑ ❑ ❑ ❑ ❑ ❑ ❑ ❑ ❑

Moon Over Down Under

Remember, the opera in Sydney, too, ain't over until the fat lady sings

TORSTEN BLACKWOOD/AFP/GETTY

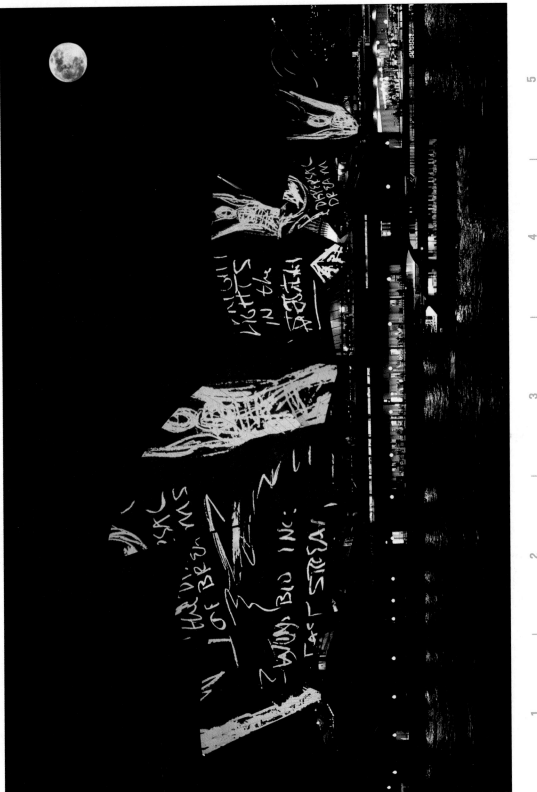

14
changes

KEEP
SCORE

⌛
5min 15sec

Answers
on page 381

GENIUS

[Finding a single difference
in these puzzles is a
challenge. Finding them all
might be impossible.]

Pedestrian Crosswalk

He knows enough to wait for the light

LISA MAREE WILLIAMS/GETTY

A

B

C

D

E

1   2   3   4   5

13 changes

KEEP SCORE

4min 25sec

Answers on page 382

Dizzy Yet?

It's like riding inside a very large washing machine. A top-loader.

5

4

3

2

1

A | B | C | D | E

14
changes

KEEP
SCORE

❏
❏
❏
❏
❏
❏
❏
❏
❏
❏
❏
❏
❏
❏

⧗
5min 5sec

Answers
on page 382

Fixer-Uppers

They may look a bit shabby,
but just think of the resale potential

A

B

C

D

E

1   2   3   4   5

15
changes

⏳
5min 15sec

Answers
on page 382

KEEP SCORE ★ ❏ ❏ ❏ ❏ ❏ ❏ ❏ ❏ ❏ ❏ ❏ ❏ ❏ ❏ ❏

Iron Chef

You need a stomach of steel for his chow

A

B

C

D

E

1   2   3   4   5

16
changes

5min 25sec

Answers
on page 382

KEEP SCORE ★ ❏ ❏ ❏ ❏ ❏ ❏ ❏ ❏ ❏ ❏ ❏ ❏ ❏ ❏ ❏ ❏ ❏

A Favorable Wind

One photo isn't getting quite as much lift

1

2

3

4

5

6

2min 30sec

Answer
on page 382

PHILIPPE HUGUEN/AFP/GETTY

On a Wing and a Prayer

Plane truth: Only five of these are the same

1

2

3

4

5

SHAUN CURRY/AFP/GETTY

6

2min 45sec

Answer
on page 382

In-Flight Dining

Did you know that food is less caloric at altitude?

SEAN GALLUP/GETTY

16
changes

KEEP
SCORE

❏ ❏ ❏ ❏ ❏ ❏ ❏ ❏ ❏ ❏ ❏ ❏ ❏ ❏ ❏ ❏

⧗

5min 55sec

Answers
on page 382

A | B | C | D | E

1   2   3   4   5

Cheek to Jowl

It's one way of making new friends

A

B

C

D

E

1   2   3   4   5

16
changes

KEEP
SCORE

⌙ ⌙
⌙ ⌙
⌙ ⌙
⌙ ⌙
⌙ ⌙
⌙ ⌙
⌙ ⌙
⌙ ⌙
⌙ ⌙
⌙ ⌙
⌙ ⌙
⌙ ⌙
⌙ ⌙
⌙

⌛

5min 15sec

Answers
on page 382

Right of Way

This would be the wrong time for a mechanical mouse to show up

JIM DYSON/GETTY

20
changes

KEEP
SCORE

6min 35sec

Answers
on page 383

A

B

C

D

E

5   4   3   2   1

LIFE
CLASSICS

[
These puzzles were
specially created with
memorable photos
from the LIFE archives.
]

Will Work for Peanuts

Because there is no elephant minimum wage

A

–

B

–

C

–

D

–

E

1 | 2 | 3 | 4 | 5

10
changes

KEEP
SCORE

❑
❑
❑
❑
❑
❑
❑
❑
❑
❑

⧗

2min 45sec

Answers
on page 383

Strategic Air Command

These future aviators of America have big dreams

CHARLES STEINHEIMER/LIFE

A

—

B

—

C

—

D

—

E

1   2   3   4   5

11
changes

⏳
4min **10**sec

Answers
on page 383

Aqua-Cat

He bravely goes where no feline has gone before

A

–

B

–

C

–

D

–

E

1 | 2 | 3 | 4 | 5

9
changes

KEEP
SCORE

2min 15sec

Answers
on page 383

Heaven's Angels

The boys are eating their dust

LOOMIS DEAN/LIFE

A
—
B
—
C
—
D
—
E

1 | 2 | 3 | 4 | 5

12
changes

⧗

4min 35sec

Answers
on page 383

KEEP SCORE ★ ❏ ❏ ❏ ❏ ❏ ❏ ❏ ❏ ❏ ❏ ❏ ❏

Under the Big Top

It's the greatest show on the third rock from the Sun

RALPH MORSE/LIFE

A
—
B
—
C
—
D
—
E

1   2   3   4   5

9
changes

⧖
3min 50sec

Answers
on page 383

KEEP SCORE ★ ❑ ❑ ❑ ❑ ❑ ❑ ❑ ❑ ❑ ❑

[ANSWERS]

Finished already? Let's see how you did.

[INTRODUCTION]

Page 261: Jumping for Joy . . .
No. 1 (A2): This horsey's ear is getting just a bit larger. No. 2 (A4 to C4): These lights don't need no stinking tower. No. 3 (B3): Four-legs may not know it, but two-legs's reign ended with the snapping of the reins. No. 4 (B4): Flapping in the breeze has stretched out this flag. No. 5 (C2): The wind seems to have changed direction. No. 6 (C3): A hoof has hoofed its way out of the image. No. 7 (D4): The spoke has delusions of wooden grandeur. Nos. 8 and 9 (E1): The gardeners have planted another shrub, while the number sign has had its last countdown.

[NOVICE]

Page 263: Baa, Baa, Yellow Sheep No. 1 (A4): Can you see the fridge now? No. 2 (B1 to B2): It's a sure sign of reversal. No. 3 (B3): They need to repost the poster. No. 4 (B5): That's what we call back to the future. No. 5 (C1): She's either turning the other cheek or shaking her head at the whole sorry parade. No. 6 (E2): This one seems to have an invisible hoof. No. 7 (E4 to E5): It's just like dyeing an Easter egg, but how do you dip the sheep?

Page 264: Head Shot No. 1 (A1 to A2): The kiosk is in the purple these days. No. 2 (A3): Don't count on getting more than one photo from this booth. No. 3 (A3 to B3): The reflection is now just a flection. No. 4 (A4): Gee, what's holding up the roof? No. 5 (B1 to B2): This shot looks familiar somehow. No. 6 (C2 to D2): It's good to take a stand, just not this stand. No. 7 (C3): She's bucked off her buckle. No. 8 (D1 to D2): His shirt sleeve is peeking out. No. 9 (E4): The cable snakes inside the stand.

Page 266: I, Robot No. 1 (B2 to D4): This 'bot must have growing pains. No. 2 (B3): All these changing acronyms are very confusing. No. 3 (C3): Is it a good sign that the wing on his abdomen now points up? No. 4 (E1): They're cutting back the lighting to save on the electric bill. No. 5 (E3): That's also why the lights are going off in the city. No. 6 (E5): But just in case the darkness causes any unrest, they've beefed up security.

Page 268: One-Trick Pony No. 1 (A5): The lights start going on automatically at dusk. Nos. 2 and 3 (B1): The nose knows that there's one ring less. No. 4 (B3): How does he bend his foot down like that? No. 5 (C3 to D4): Changing the color of your shirt while hanging upside down from a horse—now that's a trick. Nos. 6 and 7 (D5): As the horse lost a hoof, the post must have slipped backward.

Page 270: Sky Jockey No. 1 (A1): The release handle has been skyjacked. No. 2 (B1): You've heard of hair extensions? Well, this is a wing extension. Nos. 3 and 4 (B5): Careless, careless. This plane has lost both a logo and a wing. Nos. 5 and 6 (C2 to D2): We've taken away a reflection but given the planes a longer runway. No. 7 (C3): A crooked smile is part of her charm. No. 8 (C4): When the blood rushes to your brain, colors may seem to change. No. 9 (D3): Flipping numbers are another sign of upside-downitis.

Page 272: As He Takes Flight
A cross in photo No. 6 is rotating.

Page 273: Group Bliss
The bride in photo No. 4 is going to be quite upset when she realizes she's lost her tiara.

Page 274: Puttin' On the Ritz No. 1 (B1): The light is being restored. No. 2 (B4 to C4): A tourist has popped up out of nowhere. No. 3 (B5): How will they know that it's a tea room? No. 4 (C2): She's bobbled the bauble. No. 5 (C4): The mask is winking. No. 6 (C5): Someone is freshening up. No. 7 (E2): The fake sapphire has been replaced by a fake ruby. No. 8 (E5): There's a new diamond on the floor.

Page 276: Horsing Around No. 1 (A3): Now this horse is spotless. No. 2 (A4): A tree grows . . . somewhere. No. 3 (C3): We've got to rein in the disappearing stud. No. 4 (D2): Stealth leather casts no shadow. No. 5 (D4): He's tooting on a longer flute. No. 6 (E2 to E3): Ancient Hungarian proverb: Grass grows swiftly over a resting hoof.

Page 278: Must-See TV No. 1 (A3): There's no such thing as too many guns on the wall. No. 2 (B1): A painting must have fallen down. Nos. 3 and 4 (B4): The painting has slipped down, and the bison's horn is growing. No. 5 (C5): He likes watching himself on the nanny cam. No. 6 (D1): The recliner has lost its footrest. No. 7 (D2): It's a cloven hoof no more. No. 8 (D3 to D4): When the bison gets bored he starts flipping his chain.

Page 280: **Sunday in the Park . . .** No. 1 (A4): Now, that's a bad case of red-eye. No. 2 (B5): Does anyone know a good veterinary dentist? No. 3 (C3): His arm may be small but those claws are large. Where is he hiding it? No. 4 (D2 to E2): The park has these new floating signs. No. 5 (D4 to E4): Her back must be aching. No. 6 (D5): His backpack sports a mood stripe. Nos. 7 and 8 (E4): With all the hopping around, the boy seems to have lost his patch.

Page 281: **In Search of Perfect Powder** No. 1 (A2 to B1): The copter has two new spotlights. No. 2 (A2 to B2): The antenna has squirted its last message. So goes its shadow. No. 3 (B1): Gain more light, lose a blade. Oops! No. 4 (C5): This blade is trying hard to compensate for the missing one on the other side. No. 5 (D1 to E1): The mountains are on the rise. No. 6 (D4 to E4): The pole is a bit shorter now.

Page 282: **Catch of the Day** No. 1 (A2 to A3): That's a whale of a tail. Well, actually, it's a shark of a tail. No. 2 (B1): The chimney has one less stack. No. 3 (B5 to C4): Less rain will get in now. No. 4 (C3): The plumbers put in another vent line. No. 5 (D1): It's a big pane in the glass. No. 6 (D1 to E1): The door has a brand-new paint job. No. 7 (E1): Apparently, a wheel has been withdrawn. No. 8 (E2): Car logos come and go. No. 9 (E3): Knock on wood that gate is solid.

Page 284: **Guardian Angel** No. 1 (A3): Something seems to have alarmed the flying pig. No. 2 (B2): The swiped light wasn't bright, so its sudden absence won't bring on night. No. 3 (B3): The rare and diminutive third nostril is sometimes known as a nostrilette. No. 4 (C3): This little piggie's leg hopped all the way home. No. 5 (C4): Suddenly he's got a hoofier hoof. No. 6 (D1): A red interloper has slipped into this gathering of Golden Delicious apples. No. 7 (D2): A wooden pole has rising ambitions. No. 8 (D3): She likes to stick with basic black. No. 9 (D4): He likes this sweater so much he owns one in every color. No. 10 (D5): It's a high-hat garbage can. No. 11 (E3): This is what happens when you let funhouse employees paint your signs.

Page 286: **Hitchhikers in the Sky** No. 1 (A3): He must be double-jointed. No. 2 (B4 to B5): Jumpers take care! On the way down, don't get caught on the overly long tail whatchama-callit, oh, the horizontal stabilizer. No. 3 (C1): He never learned the importance of opposable thumbs. No. 4 (C2): If the dial's danger zone is no longer red, does that mean it's safe now? Nos. 5, 6, and 7 (C3): With the whatever-it's-called missing, falling may be an option (research informs us that it's the starboard stabilizer. *Great*). But don't worry, the purple goggles will help. *Right.* Still, the bin-ocular camera will capture all the action on the way down. No. 8 (C4): By the time we count to 10, that cloud better be back in place. No. 9 (D1): A rivet has bolted. No. 10 (D5): The forest road has been overgrown.

Page 288: **House of Slytherin?** Nos. 1 and 2 (A3): Watch out! Snakes always roll their eyes before they strike. And sometimes they stick out extra tongues. No. 3 (B2): The spire sticks up. No. 4 (B4): A leopard may not change its spots, but this snake can. Nos. 5 and 6 (D2): The shadow gets bigger as the sleeve gets longer. No. 7 (D2 to E2): She carries several purses with her just for occasions like this. No. 8 (E4): This slate tile has more weight. No. 9 (E5): And this little tile is missing.

Page 290: **Hold On Tight!** No. 1 (A1): The missing strut was a spare. We hope. No. 2 (A2): That's a big hoodie. No. 3 (A5 to B5): This cab is hanging on the outside of the Ferris wheel. No. 4 (B2): She's so excited, she's looking both ways. No. 5 (C1): Better get an electrician up here before sunset. No. 6 (D2): The coaster car looks a bit worried. No. 7 (D3): He thinks he's a big wheel. Oh, he is. No. 8 (E2): The bumper has extra padding now.

Page 292: **Party Girls, GOP-Style** No. 1 (A1 to B1): Mr. Chairman, Kentucky casts all 56 votes for the next President of the United States . . . No. 2 (A3 to B3): That *S* is a bit slippery. Nos. 3 and 4 (A3 to A4): The green triangle points up. No. 5 (A4): A light has blown. No. 6 (B3 to C3): She's letting her hair down. No. 7 (B4): Stick with who? Or is it whom? *Copy!* No. 8 (C4): Yeah, lost earrings are very dependable puzzle changes. No. 9 (D2 to D3): If her skirt keeps getting shorter, she may be in trouble by the end of the night. No. 10 (E4): Don't look now, but this girl is really a flamingo.

Page 294: **Hoping for the Big Bounce**

4	1
3	2

Page 295: **Superhero in Training**

4	2
1	3

Page 296: **All Eyes on Big Ben** Nos. 1 and 2 (A4): Big Ben is less pointed these days, and bigger windows are in vogue. No. 3 (A5 to B5): The louvers are doing a handstand. Without any hands. No. 4 (B3): Let's all get together and do the checkerboard flip. No. 5 (C2): It looks like they bought the third hand secondhand. No. 6 (C4 to C5): Windows are another favorite object for puzzle changes. No. 7 (C4 to D4): The metal frame is a bit greenish.

No. 8 (C5 to D5): By now you must have realized that the character *S* is a very slippery critter in puzzle-land. No. 9 (D2): The latticework on the columns is getting a bit too ornate. No. 10 (D4 to E5): It's a good thing that the missing wheel is just a fake. Nos. 11 and 12 (D5): With a little bit of effort, an *E* becomes an *L* and a ladder loses its step.

[MASTER]

Page 299: In the Pink No. 1 (A1 to B4): There's one steeple more, we must confess. No. 2 (A5): With one steeple less, that evens the score. No. 3 (B1): The tree has been efficiently depruned. No. 4 (B5): In violation of fire regulations, a chimney has been removed and is currently being held in detention, awaiting trial by a jury of its peers. No. 5 (C3): This large-eyed bunny sees all—and he's not very happy about it. No. 6 (C5): Three windows must be better than two. Nos. 7 and 8 (D1): More boats can now tie up on the farther shore, and Mr. Swivel-Hips seems surprised about it. No. 9 (D3): What's he pointing at? No. 10 (D4): Oh, he's pointing out the hovering STOP sign. No. 11 (E3): Old Pink Skin is nursing a swollen paw.

Page 300: Risky Business No. 1 (A1 to B2): And upward through the air he flew. No. 2 (A1): He's so relaxed, he has time to wave hello to family and friends. Or is it goodbye? No. 3 (B2): Many human cannon balls have twitchy feet. Well, wouldn't you? No. 4 (B5): The force of the cannon blast has blown the top right off this tree. No. 5 (D4 to E5): It's quite a solid stripe. Nos. 6 and 7 (E1): It looks like a mysterious individual both planted a new tree and sliced away the spotlight's pole. No. 8 (E4): One of the cannon's decals has been looking in the mirror too much. No. 9 (E4 to E5): In compensation, another decal has been slapped on.

Page 302: Talk About a Hybrid No. 1 (A3): The VW house's stack has slipped a bit. It must be buggy. No. 2 (A4): The new chimney is the standard two-vent model. No. 3 (B1): Skylights are easy come, easy go around here. No. 4 (B2): They're also slippery when wet. No. 5 (B2 to B3): The windshield/window has been shuttered for the evening. No. 6 (B4): The side view sports a few more louvers now. No. 7 (B5): See what we mean about skylights. No. 8 (C1 to C2): Please return the window before we have to search you for it. No. 9 (C4): The staircase is going stealth on us. No. 10 (D4): The hubcap blinders are closing. No. 11 (E2 to E3): Mind the extra step.

Page 304: When Pigs Fly . . . No. 1 (A1 to B1): He's rapidly distancing himself from this mess. No. 2 (A2): When the helmet turns green, it's time to scream. No. 3 (A4 to B4): Someone's brother has joined the team. No. 4 (B3): It looks like he's trying to flap his wings. Good luck with that. No. 5 (B4): Now who's going to time the crash? Nos. 6 and 7 (D3): This is neither the time nor place to start losing wheels or growing teeth. No. 8 (D4): Even plastic pigs can suffer from lazy eye, especially under stress. No. 9 (E1): Relax, it's just one of our standard window additions.

Page 306: On the Monkey Bars No. 1 (A1 to A2): You never know when you're going to want a bit of extra rope, do you? No. 2 (B2 to B3): If he can smile holding himself upside down in the air, he must be having fun. No. 3 (B3): That solves a knotty problem and reduces the chance of getting splinters. No. 4 (D1 to E1): The pole bars the bar. No. 5 (D2): One blocked hole has stopped the drainage flow. No. 6 (D5): The rope is out of the loop. No. 7 (E3): Either the end of this bar is invisible or someone's about to take a spill. Nos. 8 and 9 (E5): The orangutan is holding the ends together as a platform floats away.

Page 308: Ding-Dong! The Witch Is Dead No. 1 (A2): Another darn letter has contracted the irreversible reversing disease. No. 2 (A3): Thankfully, ruby slippers come in large, extra-large, and ridiculously large sizes. No. 3 (B5): Vampires stalk the streets of New York City. Watch for their reflections—or lack thereof. Makes it kind of difficult, doesn't it? Nos. 4 and 5 (C2): As a truck teeters on the edge, a man goes strapless. Or at least his bag does. No. 6 (C3): Keep your eyes on the hand. What hand? Exactly. No. 7 (C4): They'll even steal the faces off of the posters around here. No. 8 (D1): If you throw off a sandal, just keep walking. No. 9 (D2 to E2): The crack got whacked. No. 10 (D3): The witch is a little less of a heel.

Page 310: Not-So-Skinny Dipping No. 1 (B1): This umbrella seems pointless. No. 2 (C1): Lost: Tip of tail. Reward offered. No. 3 (C3): Shake a leg so the trunk can hide. No. 4 (D1): Congratulations! You've put your thumb on the change. No. 5 (D2): The pole has an automated spinning crook. No. 6 (D4): Bigger bags hold more shells. No. 7 (D5): The rope done broke. No. 8 (D5 to E5): The poncho is seaweed green. Nos. 9 and 10 (E1): Both the umbrella tip and the pants cuff are extra-long. No. 11 (E3): Salt water has shrunk his pants. No. 12 (E4 to E5): Her smock has sagged.

Page 312: Horns of Plenty No. 1 (A1): It's another of those pesky skylight changes. Our bad. No. 2 (A4): The others make fun of his featherless headgear. No. 3 (B2): Where did it go, the missing pole? No. 4 (B4): This fellow keeps double-time. No. 5 (B5): Does anyone have a needle and some thread? Perhaps an extra button? No. 6 (C3): This section of the curb has been solidified. No. 7 (D1): With his larger instrument, he really gets to horn in. No. 8 (D1 to E1): This horn has been illuminated. No. 9 (D3 to E4): The shadow rules. No. 10 (E2): Someone gets a star for effort.

Page 314: Caution! Baby (Giraffe) Onboard No. 1 (A3 to B3): She's either shaking her head no or making sure she doesn't miss anything. No. 2 (C1): The exhaust pipe twists in the breeze. No. 3 (C3 to D3): If you can read this sign, you're in trouble. No. 4 (C3): Also, did anyone run a spellchecker on it. No. 5 (D4): Ntombi is a bit south of here. Nos. 6, 7, and 8 (E1): Okay, the cab's rear light is gone, a flasher's been added to the scene, and the red flag is really red. No. 9 (E5): A car has just pulled up and parked.

Page 316: Making Like Jonah No. 1 (A3): *Quick!* From the look of the spine, this fellow needs emergency chiropractic intervention. No. 2 (A5): The column is shrinking with age. It happens to a lot of us. Nos. 3 and 4 (B5): As the upper jaw jutted forward, the lower jaw lost a loose tooth. No. 5 (C2): A man has vanished in the light. No. 6 (D1): Its short fin can no longer swim. No. 7 (D4): A bone is wrapping itself around the step ladder. No. 8 (E3): His hair is turning brown. It must be winter. Nos. 9 and 10 (E4): Without four legs, the ladder is turning yellow.

Page 318: Traffic Jam
In photo No. 2 a boat has hit rock-bottom, leaving its sail behind.

Page 319: Doggie Diplomacy
A brand-new panoramic picture window adorns the building in photo No. 6.

Page 320: And the Band Played On No. 1 (C3): When she picked her bow, she got the short end of the stick. No. 2 (C4): Forget music! He could make millions from his hair-restoration formula. No. 3 (D1): The beachcomber is making his way along the surf. No. 4 (D2): The pegbox and scroll are away on vacation. No. 5 (D3): Now she's dressed in style. No. 6 (D4): His jacket is slowly wrapping itself around him. Hint: Never buy a tux made from python skin, even if it's on sale. Nos. 7 and 8 (D5): The box has popped two pegs and this stroller looks oddly familiar. No. 9 (E3): The foam is on the roam. No. 10 (E4): The tux's tail is more available now.

Page 322: Tipping Point No. 1 (A1 to B2): After consultations with the builders, the roof has taken a new angle on things. No. 2 (A2): One of the air conditioners is on the move. No. 3 (A3): Snip, snip with the scissors, and say goodbye to the cord. Just make sure the power is off first. Or call the electrician. No. 4 (B2 to B3): There's a new shadow on that old window of mine. No. 5 (B4): Their carpenter is named Johnny On-the-Spot. No. 6 (D3): Take a peek inside. It must be furniture moving day. Be thankful you're outside. No. 7 (E1): The eucalyptus bush is growing apace. No. 8 (E3): Instead of trying to use a short fence pole, just return it to the manufacturer. No. 9 (E5): It's getting sandier outside the fence.

Page 324: Spin Cycle No. 1 (A3 to B4): It looks like he's going for the almost-impossible dreaded double-flip. Nos. 2 and 3 (B3): The spin cycle has flung off a fender while someone raised a flag. No. 4 (C1 to D1): Taller towers have more power to gaze down upon the land. No. 5 (C5 to D5): We wonder what's hidden inside the sealed arch.

No. 6 (D4 to D5): Just apply a few bricks and, voilà, a window no more. No. 7 (D5): There's someone peeking out of the open window. No. 8 (E1): If there's a media event without a cameraman, does it really happen? No. 9 (E3): The landing gear has more reach. No. 10 (E4): The copter has an unlisted call number.

Page 326: Canal Concerto
Photo No. 3 is shy one vessel.

Page 327: The Weather Outside Is Frightful
The man in photo No. 5 doesn't have a leg to stand on.

Page 328: Flipping Flapjacks No. 1 (A1 to B1): These kids are under the watchful eyes of the church. No. 2 (B3 to C3): Flip them fast enough and you'll double your reward. No. 3 (C3): The flapjack is on the rise. No. 4 (C5): It's the case of the incredible shrinking pan. No. 5 (D3): He's elbowing his way in. No. 6 (D5 to E5): This pan has vanished all together. No. 7 (E2): Hey, who ate my pancake? Nos. 8 and 9 (E3): One girl is so happy, she could just float. Oh, she is. The other lass is stepping forward.

Page 330: Moving Day

3	6
2	5
1	4

Page 331: Don't Look Down Now

5	3
1	6
2	4

Page 332: Birds Do It, Bees Do It No. 1 (A2 to B2): An arborist has been busy with shears. No. 2 (B2): She's donated her thumb to a good cause. No. 3 (B5): Somewhere someone is feasting on a giant box of chocolates. No. 4 (C1 to D2): Hemlines are lower this year. No. 5 (C3 to D3): She's a giant to her people. No. 6 (C4 to D4): This lady is a quick-change artist. Can you make a living at that? No. 7 (C5 to D5): Fewer buildings create a more pastoral feeling. No. 8 (D2): The sign has signed off. No. 9 (D3): It's a long, long, long sleeve. No. 10 (E2): Her strap has snapped. No. 11 (E4): He's slowly

subsiding into the wood. No. 12 (E5): The tree prop is in retreat.

[EXPERT]

Page 335: Some Really Great Pumpkins

5	8	2
1	7	4
3	6	9

Page 336: Stupid Human Tricks
No. 1 (A2): A street light has been removed to reduce urban light pollution. Can you see the stars? No. 2 (A3): The lazy dog's tongue lolls loosely over her lips. *Lots of laughs.* No. 3 (A5): Is it a sign that the sign is gone? No. 4 (B1 to C2): She's traded in her bag for a slimline version. No. 5 (C1): The metal bar has been bent around the wooden rail. No. 6 (C3): Don't trip on the orange stripe. No. 7 (C3 to D3): Someone's foot has beat a hasty retreat. Nos. 8 and 9 (C4): The pooch is a little leggy and a shoestring needs replacement. No. 10 (C5 to D5): Termites seem to be busily undermining this post. No. 11 (D1): The metal barrier has taken a wider stance. No. 12 (D4): Good, good, good. Play with Frisbee now, now. Frisbee now, please. No. 13 (E4): The sleeve is a smidge longer. Just a smidge.

Page 338: A Hair-Raising Competition
Nos. 1 and 2 (A2): The hat is a little less distinguished now, and so is Mr. Unibrow. No. 3 (A4): Now, this is a real top hat! Well, it's not a bottom hat, is it? No. 4 (B4): He should see things more clearly now. No. 5 (B5): He's given his hair a whirl to give it more curl. No. 6 (E1): Button's been banished. No. 7 (E2 to E4): Two numbers have swapped. No. 8 (E2): Infinity beckons. Nos. 9, 10, 11, and 12 (E4): A white dot is not, the cord's been snipped, the 7 has been mirror-fied, and the logo, if not the product, has gone green.

Page 340: Rack 'Em Up
No. 1 (A1 to A3): Isn't this lamp shade a bit bigger than necessary? No. 2 (A3 to A4): The latticework spreads like a virus. No. 3 (A5): We snapped the chain, but we did not snap the pole below. No. 4 (B1): He may be caged, but at least he's clear of the table. Nos. 5, 6, and 7 (B2): The microphone has lost its logo, a ball has bounced into view, and someone's entered the room. Nos. 8 and 9 (B4): The blue ball rolls, and a witness vanishes. No. 10 (B5): The red ball has left the table. No. 11 (C1 to C2): The chair is impaired. No. 12 (C5): He must be holding his leg out. No. 13 (D2): Another small silvery object is kaput. No. 14 (D5): Now he knows how much time he's wasting. No. 15 (E4): He's been there so long his shoe size has gone up.

Page 342: Gourds A-Plenty
Photo No. 3 is no longer in the fried chicken business.

Page 343: Be-Side Saddle
The sock in photo No. 2 is held up with Velcro.

Page 344: Spick-and-Span
No. 1 (B1): The malleable shoe art has shifted its point of view. No. 2 (B1 to B2): I'm sorry, sir, but track information is currently unavailable and will remain so for the indefinite future. Have a nice day! No. 3 (B2 to C2): He's slipped on a blue wristband. No. 4 (B3): A clown is still a clown no matter the color of his nose. No. 5 (B5): Just hang your coat . . . where? No. 6 (C2): The sock is going over to the dark side. No. 7 (C2 to D2): A shy shoe has hidden its toe. No. 8 (C3): A festive event like this calls for earrings. No. 9 (C3 to D4): She looks good in leggings of any color. No. 10 (C4): Her bangle is true-blue. No. 11 (E1): After a while there was just one tile. No. 12 (E3): It's hard to believe her shoe size could get any bigger. No. 13 (E4): Some of this strap could really be trimmed away.

Page 346: REM
Nos. 1 and 2 (A2): A reliable chimney removal and a window merge start out this eye-popping puzzle. Nos. 3 and 4 (A3 to C4): The roving eye is now wearing a green contact. No. 5 (A5): This window would rather reflect clouds. No. 6 (B1): The roof is singing the Jackie Wilson song "Higher and Higher." No. 7 (C1): Shut that window right now! Good. No. 8 (D2 to E2): His larger size will help stem the big eye roll. No. 9 (D3): Help, help! She's dropped her book. No. 10 (E1): The car has hit the road, Jack. Nos. 11 and 12 (E3): Her pants grow long as he cautiously turns around. No. 13 (E4): Where is she hiding her bag? No. 14 (E5): Here's a freebie: His shirt is purple. Well, what did you expect? It was free.

Page 348: Moon Over Down Under
No. 1 (A5): It's moonrise over the harbor. No. 2 (B1 to C1): One of the famous roof shells is suffering from inflation. No. 3 (B2 to C2): With just a sleight of hand, a *D* becomes a *B*. Gee. No. 4 (C2): The *W* has been blown away. Get it? Can you explain it to us? Nos. 5 and 6 (C4): Another light-man has joined the gang, so turn on more than one light. Nos. 7 and 8 (D2): One more lamp has been installed on the promenade and one window removed. No. 9 (D3): Lose a window, gain, well, another window. Okay, you try making these changes sometime. Nos. 10 and 11 (D5): We're down to a single dream now. Choose wisely. But at least there's an extra doorway to handle the crowds. No. 12 (E3): A reflection of light on the water has been misplaced. If you find it, let us know. No. 13 (E4): Remember the old childhood game of Red Light, Green Light? Here it's done up in lights. No. 14 (E5): The boat has a Roman nose now. Or is it a Roman bow?

[GENIUS]

Page 351: Pedestrian Crosswalk No. 1 (A3): It must have taken a really tall truck to sheer off part of this traffic light. No. 2 (B1): Don't you think these new bricks match the old ones perfectly? Nos. 3, 4, and 5 (B3): As the roof drops, the jaws snap shut, and an eye begins to glow. No. 6 (C5 to D5): Telescopic tails were unusual anatomical additions in the late Jurassic. No. 7 (D1): Hope that car didn't go too far. It's our escape vehicle. No. 8 (D2): This bumper has less opportunity to vent now. No. 9 (D3): The hubcap has been sacked. No. 10 (D4): Even an ancient dino needs its thumbs. No. 11 (D5 to E5): Big, beautiful dino seeks chunky shadow for LTR. No. 12 (E2): This *O* has filled in quite a bit. No. 13 (E4 to E5): We just love adding extra digits on critters.

Page 352: Dizzy Yet? No. 1 (A3 to B3): Guess who's skipped out on the show? Actually, we don't know her but she looked friendly enough. Nos. 2 and 3 (A4): Stripes beat poles, and orange sweatshirts morph into purple ones every time. Them's the rules. No. 4 (C1): Bald men of the world, cast off your hats! No. 5 (C2): He's got the biggest wheel in town, or at least under the tent. No. 6 (C2 to D2): Time to call out the rope repair crew. Nos. 7, 8, and 9 (C3): Better luck next time. Not only is he rolling backward, he's also lost his skull. Not in his head, silly, on his bike. Well, at least he's gained a watch. No. 10 (C5): This bike is a little hard to handle. Nos. 11 and 12 (D4): The big, black box is a little bigger now. Maybe that's why that clump of copper-colored disks—could they be coins? Whatever. Clump of sumpin'—on top has slipped around. No. 13 (D5): The reflection has lost its connection. No. 14 (E4): This fender feels quite protective of its wheel.

Page 354: Fixer-Uppers No. 1 (A1 to A2): The window is feeling the force of gravity. No. 2 (A4): It's a quadra-optic birdhouse. No. 3 (B1): Road signage theft is a problem in these parts. No. 4 (B2 to B3): The tree's shadow has been trunk-ated. No. 5 (B4): The pole vaulted in front of the bell. No. 6 (C1): You can really stretch out in this bathtub. No. 7 (C1 to D1): We dot no *i* before its time. No. 8 (C1 to E2): This sign just keeps on growing. No. 9 (C3 to C4): My, that's a long log you have. No. 10 (C4): It takes a missing leg to tip a table down. It's tippy now, but it'll soon be falling. No. 11 (D1): The arrow has been shafted. No. 12 (D2): It's a new concept in merchandising. They sell one item and then close up shop. No. 13 (D2 to D3): A can of spray paint, and what was red is now blue. No. 14 (D3): Buyer beware. This frame is a cross-piece fleece. No. 15 (D4): All together now: "Let the sun shine in!" We can't hear you. We still can't hear you. Oh, never mind.

Page 356: Iron Chef No. 1 (A1): The lamp shade's lattice frame has a slat that's slightly long. No. 2 (A2 to B2): A light's reflection has gradually lessened, and now it's completely gone. Nos. 3 and 4 (A3): The copper headdress on the robo-waiter is lopsidedly tall, and if you thought it had a hole, you'd certainly be wrong. No. 5 (A4): Two more lights, that's nice.

No. 6 (B2 to C2): There's room at the table for one more. No. 7 (B3): If you keep crossing your eyes, they're going to stay that way. That's better. No. 8 (B5): She's out of here. No. 9 (C2): What was our waiter's name again? Nos. 10 and 11 (C3): He's so happy about earning another gold blobby thingie that he's dishing out more meat. Nos. 12, 13, and 14 (C4): Our tin man appears to like the soulful sounds of Detroit, has knocked down a metal post, and has borrowed all the meat from one of the bowls. Now we know where the extra serving came from! No. 15 (C5): The steel bar has been further incised. No. 16 (D3): The reflected claw appears to be anticipating movement in its brother claw above.

Page 358: A Favorable Wind
One of the men in photo No. 3 has ducked his head behind a kite. Look closely and you'll see it's true.

Page 359: On a Wing and a Prayer
In photo No. 6 the tailpipe—well, it's not really a tailpipe . . . fuselage pipe? Okay, the pipe with all the smoke coming out of it—is an incy wincy bit smaller. We'll bet finding it was exhausting (pun intended).

Page 360: In-Flight Dining No. 1 (A2): The building's outside design is being renewed. No. 2 (A5): Say goodbye to another window. Don't worry, it's the last time in this book. No. 3 (B1): The new skylight is the two-pane model. No. 4 (B5 to C5): We made no promises about flipping windows! No. 5 (C1): This guest bears a striking resemblance to another high diner. Nos. 6 and 7 (C1 to D1): The car drove up so fast, the streetlight spun around. Nos. 8 and 9 (C2): Could there be a safety reason why the off-brand seat is empty? Never mind, what they don't know won't hurt them. As for the rest, let them drink champagne. Nos. 10 and 11 (C3): Another diner has joined the crowd, just as the chef pulls out the big whisk. *Hmm.* Maybe he doesn't like late arrivals. No. 12 (C4 to D4): That pole was a redundant support. Excuse us, we've got to leave now. No. 13 (D2): The green dot is coming down with a bad case of wanderlust. No. 14 (D4): One of these chairs provides solid back support. No. 15 (D5): A chimney has toppled into the park. No. 16 (E2 to E3): Someone's been soldering in the hollows in the beam.

Page 362: Cheek to Jowl No. 1 (A2 to B2): An all-green shoe removes any risk of unintended product placement—and has quite a lovely Irish Spring appearance as well. (We hope our check is on the way.) No. 2 (A2): Hiked-up socks are so attractive—*not*. Nos. 3 and 4 (A3): The junction box is now well-screwed, but without a clip, the BX cable may swing. No. 5 (A4): Don't worry, he's got his thumb on the problem. No. 6 (B2 to B3): The greenish hue appears to be spreading from shoe to shoe. No. 7 (C3): After a stunt like this, it's a well-deserved star. No. 8 (C3 to D3): Polydactyly is somewhat impractical unless the offending digit can move around. If fully functional, it may have merit, as any 12-fingered pianist will attest. No. 9 (C4): It's not very polite to prefer a foot over a face. No. 10 (C4 to C5): Brickwork yet again. *Yawn.* No. 11 (D2): It may

be a bit more subtle, but it's still just two more blocks. Or rather, one. Okay, yes, a brick, a brick. Nos. 12 and 13 (D3): A knee just wants to be free, and that's what they call deep soul. No. 14 (E3): The mortar has been routed away. Nos. 15 and 16 (E3 to E4): With those extra stripes, what would you make that to be, a size 11 or 12?

Page 364: Right of Way No. 1 (A2 to B2): Without something to prop it up, the canopy above must soon recline. No. 2 (A5): Falling urns might be considered an architectural danger. No. 3 (A5 to B5): We lied about the windows. No. 4 (B3): The building is getting a facelift. No. 5 (B5 to C5): New shades are also being installed. No. 6 (C1): If I were you, I wouldn't trust that rail. No. 7 (C1 to C2): You don't have to visit Moscow to see a red square. No. 8 (C3): This lamp can't be topped. No. 9 (C4): This tusk was made for jutting. No. 10 (C5): The sphere is balling up. No. 11 (D1): When the stone slab shifted, it must have cracked. No. 12 (D2): In a dramatic reversal of entropy, the wooden leg has grown together. Soon, ice cream colds will spontaneously get colder and messy boys' rooms will clean themselves. Dream on. Nos. 13 and 14 (D3): A defiant *E* faces the other way, as an awning takes advantage of the chaos to claim more territory. No. 15 (D4): The traffic lights are putting out contradictory signals. Nos. 16 and 17 (E1): While someone's suddenly gone bald, another man is the face *not* in the crowd. No. 18 (E3): Now, this *is* the face in the crowd. No. 19 (E3 to E4): The subway isn't public anymore. No. 20 (E4): It's either reverse entropy again or someone is about to make a fortune with a baldness cure.

[LIFE CLASSICS]

Page 367: Will Work for Peanuts No. 1 (A3): One flag down, nine more to go. No. 2 (A5): What's the point in racing toward a seeple? No. 3 (B1): This sign makes lots of weak promises. No. 4 (B2): Someone must think large posters get more attention. They probably do. No. 5 (B4): The dome gets the (new) point. No. 6 (C2 to D2): It does no good to shake a stick at an elephant. Canes don't work either. We've tried. No. 7 (E1 to E2): There are more stairs there. No. 8 (E2): Scandalous—she's showing off a little boot. No. 9 (E3): Luckily only the shadow lost her head. No. 10 (E5): It's just a shadow of a tail.

Page 368: Strategic Air Command No. 1 (A4): Little Jack Horner decided not to stick out his thumb after all. No. 2 (B3 to C3): He's quietly reaching for one of the planes. No. 3 (B3): The plane seems eager to be caught. No. 4 (B5): Don't worry. He hasn't lost a foot, he's just slipped it in under the table. Probably. No. 5 (C1 to D1): How do you pull open the drawer now? No. 6 (C1 to D2): His hair auditioned for a new part. Nos. 7 and 8 (C4): One plane is showing off its wider wings, while the other has scared off its own shadow. No. 9 (E3): We won't make any promises, but these are the last missing buttons in the book. We promise. No. 10 (E4): He taps his fingers when he's restless. No. 11 (E5): Someone's dad is going to be mad when he finds out about the broken tools.

Page 370: Aqua-Cat No. 1 (A2 to A3): Note: 1 plus 1 makes 11. It's the *new* new math. Nos. 2 and 3 (B1): As *X* takes a little spin, a feline brother takes a look through the porthole. No. 4 (B3): Before they embark on their mission, somebody needs to put the *N* back in NAVY. No. 5 (B4): And fix that *V* at the same time. No. 6 (B5): Need a tip? We've got one we stole from this photo. Also, buy high and sell low. No. 7 (C3): The stitching has worn away. No. 8 (C3 to C4): He's a cool, cool cat. No. 9 (E5): The slab is shorter than it was yesterday.

Page 372: Heaven's Angels Nos. 1, 2, and 3 (B2): Let's peel off three quick answers: Rogaine or rug? Only his hairdresser knows for sure. This fellow's hair is blowing in the wind. And he appears to have headlight envy—now fixed. Nos. 4 and 5 (B3): Of course she's the leader, she's the one with the big hair. But he had to look away. No. 6 (B4): I feel the sign move under my feet. Wait, that makes no sense. Still, the sign is moving. No. 7 (C1): Here's hoping she doesn't need to stop suddenly. Or ever. No. 8 (C2): She doesn't just have a handle on things, she's got it covered. The handle, we mean. No. 9 (C3): She doesn't just lead the gang, now she lights the way. No. 10 (D1): This lady must have been recently bitten. She's going vamp on us. Nos. 11 and 12 (D5): Not only does she need a fender vendor now, she's also going to have a hard time staying within the lines.

Page 374: Under the Big Top No. 1 (A1 to A2): Maybe the acrobats can fix that light while they're up there swinging around. No. 2 (B2 to C2): In case of trouble, he can just grab the rope. But what is she going to do? Nos. 3 and 4 (B3): The swing looks a bit dodgy, but never mind. It's her outfit that's getting all the attention. No. 5 (C1 to E2): Here's a chimp who is clearly on the move. No. 6 (C3): Let's give him a really big hand. Oh, we did. No. 7 (D1 to D2): The position of the curtain seems a little uncertain. No. 8 (D2): When are they going to get that horse back in harness? No. 9 (D4): These rings are definitely unparalleled.

A Devilish Cycle

This rider is going nowhere fast

MICHAEL URBAN/AFP/GETTY

11
changes

KEEP
SCORE

3min 35sec

A
—
B
—
C
—
D
—
E

1   2   3   4   5

Solve this and become a true puppet, I mean, puzzle master.

ANSWERS No. 1 (A2): The end of the pipe has been capped. **No. 2 (B2):** There's been a tube switcheroo. **Nos. 3 and 4 (B3):** The flag has been restriped and stretched. **No. 5 (C3):** This U won't hold water. **No. 6 (C5):** If they keep growing, his devilish horns will need to be filed down. **No. 7 (D3):** An extra spoke won't help this contraption get going. **No. 8 (D4):** Oh, no. It's thumbs down. **No. 9 (D5):** The roses are blowing backward in the breeze. **No. 10 (E2):** The barn is windowless. **No. 11 (E5):** With all the pumping, his sneaker has earned its extra stripe.